The Rest of the Man's Show

A beautiful, gritty story and guide to bring new life to your soul

Bill LaMorey

Published by Rest of Your Show Media

Edited by Susan Andres

ISBN 9798992583410

Printed in the United States of America

Contents

Dedication

To the girl in the tent.

With deep love and boundless gratitude to my family, friends and everyone who believed in me, helped me along the way and bet on the long shot. You are in the heart of this book even if not mentioned by name.

And to the other long shots out there, I'm cheering you on.

Prelude

Cold sweats riddled my nauseous, aching body as the flu-like symptoms screamed, demanding more of the poison I was withdrawing from. As my body shook in agony, my soul felt even more beyond redemption. Lost, confused, hopeless, and purposeless, with no sense of what to do after detox. Maybe I should have taken a little more in that last shot as a final misery cure. Yet, there I was, hoping against hope to pull through and find brighter days. Maybe I'd have a little apartment in Miami with a blue-tongued chow chow, excited when I came home, keeping me company while I listened to music and ate takeout Thai food. It wasn't much, but it was something to dream about as an escape from the nightmare I had made of my life.

The Miami apartment was never to be; my vision was too small. I couldn't have imagined God's plans to rescue me from brokenness and redeem my life in unimaginable ways. How could I have believed I would someday lead a residential recovery ministry? Or comprehend the beautiful family God would entrust me to lead and share life with? And who would have guessed that this lost soul would eventually start a church to help other broken people find hope, purpose, and community? Certainly not me, and yet it all happened.

This book bridges the gritty and beautiful gap between those two paragraphs you just read. I didn't write this book just to tell my story; I wrote it to also help you tell yours. By sharing my journey of redemption, I aim to inspire you and offer the guidance I've learned along the way. I don't write as a "Pastor Expert" with all the answers but as someone who pulls back the curtain on the dark places in my life and invites you to do the same with yours. I'll guide you through the redemptive circles of my life, helping you see and celebrate your areas of redemption and identify where there's still work to do.

The book's second half transitions from story to guide, exploring specific practices you can pursue for healing and growth. I don't know your story, but I believe something bigger and better than you ever dreamed is available to you, too—a life that would make your jaw drop if you could see it now. I wrote this book to expand your vision, build your faith, guide you toward greater wholeness, and help you launch into an exciting new chapter of your story. What will the rest of your show look like?

Introduction

After a Sunday morning church service, a woman approached me, introduced herself, and, surprisingly, said, "I bat for the other team." I forced a polite smile, bracing for what I assumed would be an awkward conversation. After a pause, she clarified, "I'm Jewish." I was intrigued.

She explained she had attended our church to witness the dedication of her friend's baby girl. Although her original plan was to leave immediately after the ceremony, her 4-year-old son insisted on staying, saying, "I want to see the rest of the man's show." That made me grin.

Expecting a confrontation, I was caught off guard when the woman complimented me instead. She shared that her son had repeated my three main points perfectly. "You kept his attention the entire time," she said, "and he understood everything you said."

I thanked her sincerely, deeply touched by her kind words. At that moment, I mentally locked in the title of a book I knew I'd write someday, even though I had no idea what its content would be.

Since you're reading this, I assume you're older than 4 or, at the very least, as sharp as that little boy. Regardless, I hope this book engages you and provides inspiration, clarity and guidance. Let me explain the title, the structure, and how it might help you.

Many see me as a clean-cut pastor and assume I grew up in a Christian home, went to seminary, and transitioned directly into pastoral work. But my story is far grittier, wilder, and more beautiful than they might expect.

In **Act I**, I'll share my story in a raw and revealing way. Each chapter explores themes of brokenness—some may resonate with your own experiences, some might bring tears, and others laughter. I don't laugh because I take these moments lightly but because humor is a part of who I am.

In **Act II**, I'll share the redemptive arc of my story—how God's transformative power changed my life. This section will get to the deeper meaning of the book title: *The Rest of the Man's Show*. Too many people fail to experience the incredible things God has in store for them. I hope this part inspires you to stick around for the rest of *your* story and step into the life He designed for you.

Finally, in **Act III**, I'll provide actionable healing practices I've learned. These come from books, 12-step programs, churches, conferences, rehabs, and even my time in jail. Each practice comes with steps you can take to change the trajectory of your life. You can read this section chronologically or skip to the most relevant parts. It will be worth it if even one practice helps you move from brokenness to experiencing God's healing presence in your life.

So, whether you're a skeptic, seeker, believer, or somewhere in between, my hope is the same: that you'll see the rest of *The Man's* show and experience the transformative power of God's love in your own life.

Now, without further ado, I pull back the curtain and invite you behind the scenes to experience *The Rest of the Man's Show*.

Chapter 1—Roots

In the summer of 1971, in Norwich, Connecticut, William Huntington LaMorey Jr. came into the world. While my grandfather shared the name William H. LaMorey, the more distinguished title of "the Third" eluded me because his middle name differed from mine. When I was old enough to understand, I learned the story behind my unique middle name. It came from my grandmother, Margaret "Peggy" LaMorey, whose maiden name was Huntington. Wanting to preserve her cherished family name after marrying into the LaMorey family, she passed it on to my father, who, in turn, passed it on to me.

The name Huntington held a special place in our family because it connected us—albeit distantly—to Samuel Huntington, a signer of the Declaration of Independence and, according to some (especially my family), the first true President of the United States. This family pride rubbed off on me, and years later, I hung a framed copy of the Declaration of Independence on my office wall—not just to honor the birth of our nation but also to subtly brag about my "royal roots" to anyone who would pay attention.

My mother, Frances, is the middle child of three daughters born to Cecile and Frank. While my mom's family didn't have a famous ancestor to boast about, her father, Frank (whom we called Pepere), was a legend in his own right. A lively character, Pepere proudly dubbed himself the "King of the Reelers" at the textile factory in Plainfield, Connecticut, where he worked and eventually retired. If you ever meet me, ask about Pepere stories—I promise they'll have you laughing!

My Italian stallion grandfather and French-Canadian grandmother (Memere) divorced when I was too young to notice. Still, he would visit periodically during my childhood, often bringing gifts of bath foam and soaps from his girlfriend, "the Avon Lady." He had a nickname for everyone, including my mother, whom he affectionately called Fatty Booch (she wasn't fat) and later Little Iodine (apparently, she was often injured).

If I had to give my mom a nickname, it would be St. Frances. She is one of the kindest people I've ever known. Despite enduring countless challenges, she radiates an incredible smile and a laugh so infectious it can warm up any room. I am eternally grateful to her. As a single mom, she set a wonderful example, made enormous sacrifices, never stopped believing in me, and shaped me in countless ways. (I could've done without inheriting the short genes—thanks, Mom!) The older I get, the more I realize how difficult those single-mother years must have been, especially when I was older and completely out of control. Yet, despite the challenges, those were the best years of my childhood.

Though absent for much of my life, my father had a disproportionately large influence on me during our limited time together. I'll delve into his story in the next chapter. As an only child, I didn't have siblings but was lucky to grow up with some wonderful cousins, aunts, and uncles.

I have no memories of my parents together—no dinners around the table, no shared holidays. They divorced when I was around 2. My parents' split mirrored the experiences of many of my "latchkey kid" Gen X friends as the Boomer generation experienced skyrocketing divorce rates. Without my dad, my earliest and happiest childhood, preteen, and teen memories were just my mom and me. An unwelcomed interruption would bring pain and chaos into our lives, but I'll also save that story for the next chapter.

Although my family boasts a historical figure on my dad's side and a legendary character on my mom's, I've learned that, like most families, ours had much going on beneath the surface. As I share these stories, I want to emphasize that I write without judgment, bitterness, or anger. My family did their best with the tools and resources they had.

Still, there was deep brokenness and pain, particularly on my father's side, that many in my family were not equipped to process. These unaddressed wounds often led to destructive coping mechanisms like substance abuse and addiction. Both my grandmother and grandfather were alcoholics, as was my father. My uncle Al struggled with addiction to speed and other drugs.

I started noticing these behaviors at a young age, and they unsettled me so much that I swore I would never touch drugs or alcohol. If only Little Billy had stuck to that promise.

Chapter 2—Father

It took me many years to understand the importance of having a father actively present and how profoundly his absence shapes you. Growing up, I knew I wanted a father. Technically, I had one, but he wasn't in my life long enough to make much of a difference—like passing down his tall genes.

My father wasn't around for my birth; he was on assignment with the Navy in the Mediterranean. A year later, he returned, and we were a family for about six months before he disappeared again. When he finally called my mom in Connecticut from Texas, he admitted he wasn't ready to be a husband or a father. Their marriage ended when I was about 1½. I never knew him as a regular part of my family, but for a brief time, I got to know him—mostly from a distance.

Most of what I know about my father comes from family stories. Bill was fun and a bit of a character. Everybody liked him. He made people laugh. He hustled pool. Once, he fell asleep playing bass guitar during a live show. Another time, he came home drunk to the wrong house, slept on the couch, and the homeowner cooked him eggs in the morning. I loved learning everything I could about him. But more than anything, I wanted to know him personally.

11

I cherish the few memories I have with my dad. Once, he took me to a carnival rodeo, but we ran out of gas and had to hitchhike home. (He may not have always been very responsible.) Watching '60s Batman reruns at his apartment is another fond memory. My favorite was when he bought me a King Kong model, and we built it together. I went outside roaring like King Kong, chasing some neighborhood kids. One boy didn't find my antics amusing, so he punched King Kong, shattering it. My growls turned into tears, and I ran back to my father in distress. He came out, helped me gather the broken pieces, and repaired it as best he could—my hero. Then everything changed.

One morning, as I was getting ready for kindergarten, I came downstairs and found my mother wailing. She sat me down and told me my father had died in an accident. How does a 5-year-old even begin to process that? I told her I needed to get ready for school, but she told me I was staying home. We sat in the apartment and cried. What I remember most is watching my mother cry agonizing tears. My dad had always been distant, but now the distance was permanent. He was gone, leaving a shadow that would always hang over my life.

My mother remarried when I was 6. Her new husband was an artist—and a con artist. While he painted, he rarely worked, which stood in stark contrast to my mother, who was the steadfast breadwinner of our family. When anger and intoxicants got the best of him, he took it out on her. I vividly remember his punching her in the face. She was everything to me, and he treated her like she was nothing. I was so furious I wanted to kill him, but I was powerless.

While he never physically abused me, he was often verbally abusive, especially when drunk or high—which was much of the time. I remember my mother counting the cash left in his jean jacket pockets after he'd drained her bank account to fund a night of partying. Once, on Christmas Day, he knocked over the tree in a rage. That moment shook me as much as he shook the tree. You get the idea, constant chaos.

One thing I grudgingly credit him for happened after he married my mother. I told him I'd be willing to change my last name to his for family unity. He told me to keep my name. I felt relieved, even now, though I also felt ashamed for being willing to give it up. We'll come back to shame.

One of the most poignant father-figure moments of my childhood intersected the narratives of my birth father and stepfather. When I was 10, I met a 14-year-old named Freddie, who was always in trouble. For a brief time, he mentored me in bad behavior—shoplifting, raising money for fake charities, and other mischief. One Saturday morning, he convinced me to break into his middle school. (I was in third grade.) He somehow acquired keys to the building. We vandalized classrooms, wrote on chalkboards, and made tuna sandwiches in the Home Ec room. Some girls saw us, turned us in, and soon, I was in the DA's office.

The DA scared me straight, detailing the consequences I could face. Having seen *Over the Edge*, I was convinced I'd end up on a prison bus to juvie. Thankfully, the DA gave me a stern warning and let me go. That marked the end of my friendship with Freddie.

Later that day, my stepfather asked, "Do you want to become like your father?" I recited the story I knew: my father had died in an accident. That's when he dropped a bombshell. My dad had a criminal mentor of his own. He befriended a man in jail while serving time for drunk and disorderly behavior. After their release, they partnered to rob liquor stores along the coast of Connecticut, taking turns between driving and robbing. On my dad's turn to go in, the store owner shot and killed him.

I sat in stunned disbelief, overwhelmed by sorrow and shame. Anger soon followed—not at my father, but at the man I hated for using this revelation against me. Relief came a year later when my mother and stepfather divorced. At 11, I finally felt free of another man in the house.

Growing up, I didn't think much about my father's absence daily, but it was always there. When I needed guidance, I wished I could turn to him. When I achieved something cool, I longed to hear, "Son, I'm proud of you." Much later, I realized how badly I had needed his discipline and redirection. My mom gave me all the love I needed—and more—but I missed the balance a father could have provided.

Every Father's Day, I sorted through a box of his belongings: old photos, letters, his pocket watch, military dog tags, and his wallet. Inside the wallet, there's a $5 bill and a cutout of the Land O'Lakes lady, modified so her knees look like breasts when you lift the flap. It never failed to make me laugh through my tears.

Now and then, I visit my father's humble grave next to his father's. It's sobering to look down at the name we share— William H. LaMorey—on two gravestones and contemplate their lives. Did they enjoy life? Had they wanted more? The abandoned Old Trinity Church and gated graveyard where they lie in Brooklyn, Connecticut, are supposedly haunted. I don't know if that's true, but I know my father isn't doing the haunting. That ghost has been far too busy haunting me.

Chapter 3—Trouble

My mom, who might be biased, always says that despite my mischief, I was kind. I appreciate that and hope it's true, but it makes me wonder: Am I the worst good guy or the best bad guy? That philosophical question is one for another day. While I never meant to hurt anyone, I often acted without thinking and found myself in trouble.

Do you remember your first memory? What is it? I hope it's something that makes you smile. Want to guess mine? That's right—getting into trouble! It was the '70s, and nearly everyone smoked cigarettes (often the funny ones, too), including my mom. I didn't share their enthusiasm, so my first memory is Little Billy sitting on the living room couch in front of a mountain of tobacco. I'd proudly made it by unwrapping all my mom's cigarettes—my first masterpiece of mayhem. I don't remember what my mom said, but her tone was loud and angry as she not-so-joyfully ushered me to my room.

Another time, I disappeared, and my terrified mom called the police while frantically searching for me. After a couple of hours, the cops found me hiding under my bed. My mom asked, "Why didn't you say anything?" I don't remember my response, so you'd have to ask her.

At 6, I decided to poison my mean babysitter. I whipped up a deadly potion of Alka-Seltzer, toothpaste, and who knows what else, then offered it to her in a glass of water. Thankfully, she was smart enough not to drink it. OK, maybe that wasn't very kind. Where does a kid even get an idea like that? Tom & Jerry?

But not all my antics were dark. When I was 9, I wore my Batman Underoos over jeans, tucked a cape towel into my T-shirt, and patrolled the neighborhood to fight crime. Maybe that balances the scales a little.

Growing up, I loved to read—mostly comic books, but regular books, too. I thrived on learning until I got bored. That's when I'd pivot from studying to causing trouble. In elementary school, I was the class clown and regularly got sent to the principal's office to see my good friend, Mr. Drag. My teacher, Mrs. Larkin, constantly told me, "Boy, you run my blood pressure up." One time, I accidentally started a massive food fight in the cafeteria by lobbing a carton of sour milk behind me like a dairy missile and soaking someone. The victim threw stuff back, causing chaos and a terrible mess for the custodians to clean up.

Middle school was more of the same. After a kid punched me in the face for no reason shortly after school started, my mom transferred me to a Christian school. The principal, Mr. Talent, soon became my new disciplinarian. I got in trouble for punching a classmate, Patrick, in the stomach after he kept telling me the *Return of the Jedi* spoilers before I got to see it; I'd warned him!

Eventually, the principal gave me a choice: be expelled or be "graduated" six weeks before 8th grade finished if I agreed not to return. I chose the latter.

Trouble followed me to public high school. Skipping class, disrupting lessons, and occasional fights earned me detentions and suspensions. My frequent visits to the principal's office led to an unusual punishment: doing administrative work, like writing call slips to summon students to the principal's office. On one occasion I may or may not have forged a few for my friends, called them out of class, and left with them to meet Ozzy Osbourne at a record store for autographs.

My friends and I went on many "adventures." When I was growing up, times were so different from today. We didn't have digital trackers or cellphones, so we enjoyed the freedom to roam wild in packs. It was common for us to be out all day riding our bikes until we heard our mothers yelling for us to come home for dinner.

When I was 11 or 12, my friend George and I were on such an adventure. We were taking a shortcut through the woods in Fort Lauderdale when we encountered a pond. A long pole laid over the water, so we walked across it. Everything was fine until George lost his balance, fell, grabbed me, and pulled us into the water. I soon discovered that George had worse balance than I and couldn't swim. What should have been an annoying, wet moment became my first near-death experience. Whenever I tried to pull my head above the water, a panicked George would clutch onto me, dragging me back under. My life flashed before my eyes: my mom's smiling face, random events, and scenes, including Pepere playing with a toy helicopter with me on the lawn.

I'd heard that drowning victims go down three times, and I was certain I was about to die. But something screamed inside me, "This can't happen; I want to live! What if my mom never knows what happened to me?" So, in a fight for my life, I kicked George in the nuts as hard as I could. I remember his shocked face and his reaching down. While momentarily distracted and with his hands off me, I swam away from him as fast as possible to the shore. Fortunately, necessity taught George he could swim, and we both survived the day.

At 15, I had another brush with death at a David Lee Roth concert. My friends and I brought along a bottle of Jack Daniels. I drank it like beer, knowing nothing about hard liquor. My memories of that night are blurry: buying a T-shirt, walking into the bathroom, and passing out on the filthy floor. An ambulance took me to the hospital, where I woke to my poor mother and a stern nurse informing me that my stomach had been pumped. They said one more shot would've killed me. My mom grounded me for a month, leaving me alone in my room with my TV, VCR, record player, and books. When I returned to school, all the rock and metal kids wore concert T-shirts with "Roth Rules" on their backs. I had to take their word for it.

I wish I could say my run-ins with the law ended after my incident with Freddy, but they didn't. One time, my friend Al and I were smoking pot on the beach in Hollywood, Florida, when the cops caught us! They gave us a choice: pick up the trash or go to jail. We cleaned the beach. Walking home, we passed a police boat, and for no good reason, I flipped them off—maybe even a double-bird. The officers weren't amused. They started maneuvering their boat to the shore, but we laughed, figuring we had plenty of time to outrun them. As we began our escape, luck was not on our side. The bridge went up, delaying our getaway. When the police officers hit the shore, they unfolded their bikes and caught up to us. That was probably the hardest someone has ever slapped me. Did I deserve it? Probably. Was it right? Probably not. But hey, I started it—like most of the trouble that came my way.

Chapter 4—Escapism

Early in our marriage, my wife went shopping while I played a video game on our living room computer. When she came back, she was surprised to find me still playing. "How long have you been playing?" she asked. I guessed about an hour, which seemed right. She then said, "I've been gone over 2.5 hours!" Oops— typical me!

Growing up, I loved comic books. Batman was amazing, especially since his archenemy, the Joker, was the greatest comic villain ever! But Marvel was my main escape, especially through my favorite character, Spider-Man. The deeper appeal was the hope that if a geeky teenager could become a super-cool, strong, wisecracking hero, maybe I could too. Would Mary Jane leave Peter for me? Where would I get those blue and red tights? A small part of me still hopes to be bitten by a radioactive spider.

Guided by my older neighbors across the street, Tommy and Brian (sorry for losing the boot on your Mego Iron Man figure, guys), I became an avid comic collector. I had a valuable collection by my late teens. I spent hours reading comics, watching cartoons, and eventually, movies when technology caught up.

It wasn't just comics; I loved all kinds of stories. I was a big reader, always wanting more books. My mom bought me book club subscriptions, took me to the library, gave me money for Scholastic Book Fairs, and always fed my hunger for reading. I also watched a lot of TV growing up—sitcoms, dramas, game shows, and even talk shows. My TV habits went off-track at 14 when I became addicted to *The Young and the Restless* at Aunt Patty's house. As a metalhead, I couldn't let my friends know, so I had to quit in the fall. It wasn't just TV; I loved movies, too— funny, sad, scary, action-packed, adventure, and especially sci-fi. I was thrilled to see the first *Star Wars* movies in theaters, and yes, I watched *Return of the Jedi* 13 times on the big screen!

Speaking of *Star Wars*, I also feverishly collected action figures. I created endless adventures with friends, using figures, playsets, and various spaceships. (Getting the At-At one Christmas felt like winning the lottery.) I'd freeze some characters in place to create a more realistic story on my planet Hoth set. We might have taken it too far by re-creating *Friday the 13th* with action figures, but it was the '80s.

When I was 13, we were moving from one apartment to another, and a friend of my mom's told me, "Billy, it's time to grow up and put these figures away." It was the first time I had to face the end of my childhood, and I didn't want to let go. As an only child, those toys had been my constant companions, so putting them away wasn't easy. (Someone should make a movie about that.)

As I packed the toys, I moved on to other things, like video games. If you grew up in my era, you can probably still hear the sounds of classic arcades like I can. I carefully budgeted my weekly allowance to balance key priorities—buying comics and playing video games. I spent hours in arcades, even playing video poker to win more tokens so I could keep playing. Eventually, home consoles like the Atari 2600, Commodore 64, and Nintendo brought video games (albeit with lackluster graphics) into my home.

One story shows just how addicted and selfish I had become. The Vectrex was a state-of-the-art video game console with vector graphics, a built-in monitor, and a joystick, though it had the drawback of needing color screens changed for each game. I convinced my mom to buy it for me for Christmas. I begged her so relentlessly on Christmas Eve that she gave it to me that night instead of waiting until morning. The next day, after the thrill wore off, I felt hollow. I still feel guilty about it every time I remember it.

It took a lot of self-control not to make a joke about that last sentence. I'm Chandler from *Friends*, using humor to make things awkward and avoid uncomfortable feelings. Laughter has helped me through tough times. I love to laugh and make people laugh with a careful turn of phrase, a clever observation, or a funny story. (I don't tell jokes.)

In addition to watching TV sitcoms, I grew up reading *MAD* magazine, the better *Cracked*, and the even better *Crazy*. I'm convinced those magazines, Spider-Man, and Bugs Bunny helped develop my sense of humor and sarcasm. I'm quick with quips, good with impersonations, and inject humor into my stories, teaching, and even preaching. I'm also an excellent crank caller. Humor is a huge part of who I am, but it's also where I hide sometimes.

I'm also a huge music fan. (In case you're wondering, I'm listening to Al Di Meola right now, though I usually prefer to write in silence.) Audio stories with catchy beats? I'm in! As a kid, I listened to whatever pop and rock my mom played in the car. My favorite band at age 6 was Kiss. I hadn't heard their music yet, but I started collecting their trading cards because they were the coolest-looking band in the world.

I eventually became a fan of their music, though I was initially disappointed when my cousin Mickey played me one of their records. I had expected them to sound tougher. My true musical love began when I saw the *Run to the Hills* video by Iron Maiden on MTV. I rushed out to buy the album, but the artwork was too scary for 11-year-old me. When *Flight of Icarus* came out the next year, I went back and bought their entire catalog.

I still listen to almost every genre of music except country. Metal, though, became a huge part of my life. Iron Maiden was my new favorite band, and heavy metal became my go-to genre. If you'd asked me at 11 what I wanted to be when I grew up, I would have said a writer, comedian, or rock star. I took guitar lessons and played in a local band or two (ever heard of Brazen Hussy?), but I was never that good. Still, I got to be around rock stars who became famous, which you'll hear more about later. Maybe the writer thing will work out.

There's nothing wrong with comics, books, TV, movies, video games, laughter, or music (though you might not like some of their forms). But these things can become unhealthy when used to escape reality, avoid pain, and numb the soul. The drugs that came later were far more destructive, but the unhealthy escapism I practiced early on set patterns for worse habits to develop. I didn't have anyone to talk to about the tough things I'd gone through in my early years, and I didn't think I should. When life got hard, I shoved my pain down and distracted myself with whatever I could so I didn't have to face my messy life, which mirrored my cluttered bedroom full of scattered toys, books, clothes, and more.

And heaven forbid someone tried to pry. Before they knew what happened, I'd freeze them out and retreat into one of my favorite fantasy worlds. There were a few years when I didn't want to be touched, not even hugged by my mom. I didn't know why then, but now I realize it was part of keeping parts of myself hidden and retreating into the safe but lonely world of escape. Unsurprisingly, my favorite concept album is Pink Floyd's *The*

Wall—it felt like my own story. You can't get hurt if you lock everyone out, brick by brick, and stay safe behind a wall.

Chapter 5—Bodies

While I mastered the art of escaping my reality, there was one thing I couldn't escape: my body. I don't mean metaphysically—I came to hate my body over the years. Let me start by saying that I now appreciate how fortunate I am to have a body that works and is mobile. Many people face lifelong struggles with disabilities, so I am grateful to have a healthy body. But as kids, most of us don't think like that. We notice our flaws in mirrors and absorb the opinions of others. Eventually, your harshest critic becomes yourself, shaped by external judgments. It's not just that something is wrong with your body; you start thinking there's something wrong with you. You're flawed, you don't measure up, and you should feel ashamed. And so you do, because you believe the criticism is a fact.

My biggest body issue was being overweight. I liked to eat and wasn't very athletic, so the combination made things difficult. I played baseball for a few years, starting with the Blue Invaders, but stopped after elementary school. Over time, I realized, "Hey, I'm kind of chubby." I was the fat kid all through my youth and into early high school. There are many challenges when you're overweight. For one, trying to look cool while shopping with your mom in the "husky" section of the department store. And then there's the ridicule of others; kids, especially my generation, can be pretty mean. Being quick-witted, I learned to fight back with insults and pretended the words didn't hurt, but they did. They dug deep and affected how I saw myself, all while I kept a smile. The embarrassment grew, and I tried to hide my body more and more. Does this loose shirt hide what I see when undressed? Do these dark colors make me look slimmer? It was hard to feel comfortable in my skin when the layers of fat were pushing it out.

The battle of the bulge has been ongoing. My body has had its ups and downs—I lose weight, and then it finds me again. I tried Weight Watchers, SlimFast, and other plans when I was young, then Body for Life, Whole30, and others later in life. For exercise, I tried Nautilus machines as a kid and went to the gym occasionally, but I never stuck with it. I finally have a consistent gym routine, but it took a long time to get there! In high school, I lost weight for a bit and maintained a skinny-fat look. As a metalhead, I felt pressure to keep my image up, and being overweight wasn't cool with the rock crowd. But I wasn't really healthy—I just learned to starve myself to avoid being the fat guy I hated.

You can control your weight, but with height, you're out of luck! My dad was 6'1", so I had high hopes for my height. With height, it's a waiting game, hoping for a growth spurt. But it didn't happen. Eventually, I accepted that my mom's genes won out, and I maxed out at 5'8". Being short gave me another reason to feel self-conscious about my body. No one wants to be the short guy. I related to Joe Pesci's character in *Goodfellas* when he says, "I wish I was big just once!" Studies show that taller men are likelier to be hired for important roles and earn more money. And girls like tall guys, too—they want to look up to you, not down. It bothered me, but in some ways, I didn't let it hold me back. I stayed optimistic and kept striving to achieve. After all, if Bruce Dickinson (who's shorter than I am) can be the lead singer of Iron Maiden, pilot their 747s, fence, and run a business, maybe I could do cool things too. Over the years, I've learned to take short jokes and jabs in stride. For example, a guy once greeted me at church after a service with, "You're much taller on the podcast." Indeed.

My body may be short, but I was determined not to let my hair be. I fought hard for long hair. I remember the pastor's daughter at my Christian middle school cutting my hair outside the sanctuary one day. She trimmed my bangs, revealed my eyes, and said, "You're really handsome under all that hair." I'd always thought I was ugly, so hearing that from a pretty girl was a shock.

Despite this, at 13, I was determined to grow out my hair, even if it meant quitting a part-time job I liked at a grocery store and negotiating with my mom. Eventually, my hair grew past the awkward phase and long enough to look "cool." While I disliked most of my body, I loved my hair and wore it long for about 10 years until I shaved it off one day. I loved how it made me look more like my heavy metal idols and less like a nerd. It also allowed

29

me to hide behind it while standing out and being different. It became a shield but also a statement of how I wanted others to see me rather than the parts of me I didn't want to show.

As I struggled with my body, my actual heart became another issue. At age 12–13, I was diagnosed with idiopathic hypertrophic subaortic stenosis (now called hypertrophic cardiomyopathy). It's a condition where the left ventricle of the heart is too thick, which affects the heart's electrical system and can cause irregular heartbeats—or even sudden death. Hearing that was terrifying. They told me that while I could exercise, I should avoid pushing myself too hard, especially with weight training. There was a chance I could die suddenly, but with caution, maybe I wouldn't. Now, I had a doctor's note excusing me from exercising!

I tried to stay calm on the outside, but inside, I was terrified. How do you deal with that at such a young age? How do you process knowing you might die suddenly at any moment? As an adult, I've learned that most people with the disease die with it rather than from it. I run, lift weights, and even used to practice Tae Kwon Do, so I don't worry about it much now. But as a kid, constantly fearing death was hard. Fat, short, and with a ticking timebomb of a heart to boot.

Chapter 6—God

I was baptized into the Catholic church shortly after birth. It must have been a special day for my family, but I don't remember it. I also have no early memories of attending church or talking about God when I was young. It wasn't a priority.

The first conversation I remember about God was after my dad died and before my mom and stepfather moved to Florida when I was 9. My uncle Al, my father's brother, was an ex-speed freak, a long-haired hippie who found Jesus and got clean through a ministry called His Mansion. We stood outside in my grandmother's backyard, and he talked to me about Jesus and how much I needed Him. I didn't understand everything he said, but as my 6-ft-plus uncle towered over me, I agreed to pray "the prayer" with him. Even though I took this step in my second significant God experience, not much happened afterward. I continued doing all the important things a young boy does. No Bible reading, prayers, church, or any of that, but a seed had been planted.

When I was about 11, my mom, desperate from her second failing marriage, called a friend who told her about Jesus, and my mom became a Christian. I mean a serious one; she jumped in with both feet and never looked back! She found a Bible-teaching church, and we were there every Sunday and many

31

other times. Her "Jesus thing" turned off my stepfather, who decided to leave shortly after. Thank you, Jesus! After a while, Tim, one of their pastors, explained the good news about Jesus to me, and once again, I prayed and asked Jesus into my life. This encounter with God was the first that led to a change. I took steps like getting baptized, inviting my friends to church, leaving Bible tracts for people to find, attending Sunday School classes, listening to some Christian music, and going to small groups in people's homes where my mom and I became enmeshed in the lives of others who also followed Jesus.

Some people in church were very good to me and my mom. One year, a couple who bought Christmas gifts for a family in need each year gave me a nice tennis racquet with my name stitched on the leather cover. (Tennis became one way I tried not to be fat for a while.) Another time, Rick, Mark, and Steve gave me my first electric guitar, a Gibson SG, and a practice amp! I was overwhelmed by their kindness in making this rock & roll dream come true. Rick even offered to give me lessons, although he refused to teach me heavy metal. Sue cut my hair for free, Scott taught me Sunday School lessons despite my mischief, Keith brought me on a TV studio tour, and Mark, an elder's son, took me in his muscle car, where I first heard "Crazy Train" by Ozzy Osbourne. Many people showed kindness to me and my mom in various ways.

At the same time, I started noticing things in church that seemed weird to me, and I began drifting away. Why did my mom and the other ladies have to wear doilies on their heads at church? Why was there organ music when no one listened to it on the radio? Did church have to be so boring? Why did people speak normally but pray in some form of Shakespearean English? Why did they let a lady sing solos when her voice made all the kids laugh and the parents squirm? All these questions became excuses as the world's allure pulled me further from the church.

For a while, I went to church with my mom out of obligation. I then fought it, but fear drew me back for a time. The church occasionally held Friday movie nights with Christian films. The ones that made the biggest impression on me were the *A Thief in the Night* series, which I classify as Christian horror. The premise of these films is that Jesus has raptured up all the Christians, and the story follows the remnant of believers who must either accept the mark of the Beast, sealing their eternal damnation, or face beheading for their faith. These films, by design, scared the hell out of me! Sometimes, when my mom was late from an evening church meeting, I became terrified that I missed the rapture. Without the internet or cell phones, I could not confirm or disprove my worst fears. So, I would call all my mom's Christian friends, hoping one would answer. My nervous fingers dialed the numbers one by one. Sue ... no answer. Phyllis ... no answer. My heart was pounding. Other Sue ... whew, she answered, and surely Sue wouldn't get left behind by Jesus, so I hung up in relief without saying a word. But at some point, lesser motives like obligation, duty, fear, guilt, etc., weren't enough to keep me going to church if I didn't want to be there, so I stopped. I still believed in God, but I didn't have much use for His church.

As an "outsider," my judgment of the church worsened. I noticed all their hypocrisy while often failing to recognize my own. My mom begged me to come, so I would show up on major holidays, and it would regularly reinforce why I didn't go most of the time. On one occasion, I heard two elderly women "whispering" behind me. "Look how long his hair is." The other replied, "He only comes on Christmas and Easter." They stopped talking when I turned around and, after looking them both in the eyes, said, "And that's my business, isn't it?" I guess I was just as judgy as they were, but weren't Christians supposed to be different?

Then, much darker matters came to light. One man who had been molesting his stepdaughter for years was sent to prison after his crimes were revealed. Additionally, an elder at the church who regularly offered to babysit kids had been molesting the boys and girls entrusted to his care. I was both thankful that I wasn't one of his victims and angry that he did such horrible things to some of the kids I considered friends. How could any person, especially an elder of the church, do such horrible things to children? How could God allow these sinister things to happen in

34

His house? These were horrific scandals with significant consequences for many lives, and they became one more reason church wasn't for me.

Over time, my shaky belief turned into agnosticism, sometimes nearly becoming atheism. I was no longer the little boy praying to Jesus with my uncle or willingly going to church with my mom. Instead, I became a rebellious teen chasing a wayward life and learning to enjoy the world's temptations so I didn't have to return to the house of God.

Chapter 7—Depression

I had learned to build my wall high and maintain it by sealing the cracks to keep everyone at a distance and limit vulnerability. However, I hadn't considered the threat of an enemy slowly growing and gaining strength from within the protected zone.

It's interesting to think about how and when you first realize you are or were depressed. It's not like using a thermometer to confirm you have a fever or seeing itchy red bumps to prove you have chicken pox. Depression is much more nebulous and trickier to diagnose. Most of us can't detect slightly declining moods and diminishing levels of happiness and joy in everyday life. After all, are you so in tune with yourself that you have a baseline of how you usually feel to measure how far off you've drifted? In my experience, you only realize you're depressed when it's so bad that it feels like a choking, dark cloud wrapped around you that you can't escape. Then, as you stabilize, you can look back at the season or cycle of depression and see the little signs and shifts that you missed as you marched right into a black soul-funk.

By nature, my personality is joyful, fun, and funny, with a hint of a stoic, darker edge just below the surface. Yet, as far back as elementary school, I sometimes got a strange feeling that would linger with me during the day. Usually, on those days, I'd come home to discover some significant drama in the family had taken place. Another big fight, another lamp smashed, and my mom upset. Some intuition? I just knew I felt "off."

During middle school, various forms of escape helped me mostly ignore any warning signs and strange feelings. As an only child, I didn't have siblings to talk to. I didn't want to talk to my mom about it, and I had a distant relationship with God, so I found ways to distract myself from unpleasant feelings.

By high school, I realized something was wrong. Some days, I felt ecstatic, like life was one grand party, and I was having the time of my life, laughing and making everyone laugh. But then, maybe the next day, a dark cloud would park over me, leaving me numb, and I couldn't wait to leave school to retreat into silent, solitary suffering. Some days, I'd turn on the TV to the static channel and stare at the screen, getting lost in the white noise. It reached the point where I would wake up in the morning feeling the heaviness of life with my first breath of air, desperately longing for peace and purpose. Though I'm not a psychiatrist, I'd say I struggled with some form of manic depression.

In my early to mid-teens, my mom took me to a Christian counselor whose office was ironically right next door to our duplex. I'm not sure what he said to her, but when he met with me, he asked me why I hated my mother. Jerk. I told him I loved my mother and he didn't know what he was talking about. He persisted, so I quickly put up another defensive layer until the session ended and never returned. Help was so close yet so far away. My mom begged me to give it another chance, but I told her that while I didn't know much about counseling, I was pretty sure the goal was to help you feel better, not worse. So, counselors were not my thing for quite a while.

As the cloud inside my soul grew to envelop me more from the outside, I turned to more potent and unconventional "medication" to get through. I had a weird friend in high school; don't feel bad for him because he knew he was strange, too. Among his oddities was the fact that he was a cutter. He would cut himself and described it as strangely enjoyable, giving him peace and well-being. With my frontal lobe not fully formed, I agreed to try this myself. For a brief season, I practiced this twisted ritual of cutting my skin with a razor to feel the warmth of my crimson lifeblood slowly draining and dripping down my exterior skin. For a season, it felt strangely cathartic and almost cleansing, but I knew it was demented and far from helpful or healthy, so I stopped. But the black days didn't stop. They would interrupt my life, paralyzing me in a twisted bundle of feelings I couldn't identify, let alone untangle. It was too much for me, and I needed to go numb. So I turned to other, stronger medicines, which made the pain go away for precious hours but also beat me down, enslaved me, animalized me, and left me in a far worse, more desperate condition than I had ever imagined.

Chapter 8—Marilyn Manson

I met Marilyn Manson (aka Brian Warner) at a Ramones concert in South Beach, Miami, in 1990. As I was leaving, a tall, skinny guy approached me and handed me a flyer for the first show of their band, Marilyn Manson & the Spooky Kids. He seemed cool, so I told him I'd check it out. The next day, I called the number on the flyer, which went to a hotline recording. I left a message, and to my surprise, he called me later that day and asked for my address. I was a little apprehensive, but I gave it to him. A few hours later, he called again and told me to go to a particular gravestone at a cemetery across the street from my home. My curiosity was greater than my creeped-out feeling, so I followed his instructions and found a little package in a plastic bag right where he said. I opened it and discovered a decapitated Barbie doll. Under that were several newspaper clippings about serial killers and gruesome murders. Under that layer was the prize: a copy of the first Marilyn Manson demo tape. I ran home to play it, and it blew me away. My tastes had by then expanded beyond metal to include punk, hardcore, alternative, and industrial music. Manson fused the best of these genres into a fresh new sound he called "Beat up your mom music." I was hooked.

While I don't want to overstate my relationship with Marilyn Manson, I'd say we became friends in the band's early years. I went to all their shows, mostly on the guest list, and helped in various ways, from operating the smoke machine to announcing the band before they came on to playing odd stage characters like an Oompa Loompa or Thing 1 or Thing 2. I hung out with the band during rehearsals and at random record store appearances. Manson also invited me to write their first interview for a local South Florida music magazine called *Tonight Today*. It was a fun honor that opened the door to continue writing for them and other music magazines. The band thanked me in the liner notes on one of their early demo tapes, *Grist-O-Line*. I was a regular on the scene, but I also spent a lot of time one-on-one hanging out with Brian and Brad (aka Gidget Gein). This time gave me a rare, fascinating front-row seat to watch the tragi-comedy of one guy becoming an international superstar and one becoming the guy who almost made it.

I saw Brian's very human, normal side. We'd go to toy conventions and geek out over rare action figures. I'd watch him deal with pre-show jitters at his mom's condo and give me his Taco Bell because he didn't want to upset his stomach before the show. We'd hang out in his room, talk about life, music, and movies, and discuss shaving stubbles that grow outside normal facial hair patterns. We went to see films like *Silence of the Lambs* (outside of which he accidentally committed Sea Monkey genocide by breaking my Sea Monkey necklace while horsing around). I saw all the usual things you'd expect from a regular person, like navigating typical relationship challenges with a girlfriend. But I also saw unique complications as girls suddenly began throwing themselves at him regularly. He was still figuring out the balance between who he was and who he was becoming. It amused me every time he called me, and my mom kept asking, "Who?" until the deep, male voice stopped saying "Marilyn" and finally relented with "Brian." He'd win that battle with the world soon enough.

Over time, Brian Warner confidently transitioned into Marilyn Manson, the character he created that became a nightmare to parents and his path to embodying all his rock & roll dreams. As the band became more popular, he became quite a local celebrity. Suddenly, your status improved simply because you were associated with the band. For me, this included getting free drinks at clubs and enjoying being in the cool kids' circle for a while. Though I didn't wear their signature style of cutoff jean shorts over spandex leggings with a lunchbox in hand, I otherwise looked the part and was often mistaken for a band member. My favorite story about this time is when I tagged along with the band to visit Zack's Rock Shop. Zack was one of the many quirky characters that made the South Florida scene so whacky and wonderful. As I admired his rock & roll merch collection, which included gigantic heads of the band W.A.S.P. from one of their tours, Zack approached me saying, "I love you guys!" He was delighted when I told him I wasn't in the band and tried to pitch me to join as a guitarist for a new local band he was managing called the Clowns. "You'd be perfect for this! They're great; they're doing something unique. They each have clown makeup on to conceal their secret identities," he explained. "You mean like Kiss," I asked. "No, no; it's totally different," he said. "It's clown makeup!" Whatever happened to the Clowns?

Don't get me wrong—Marilyn Manson used plenty of shock-value gimmicks, too. You have to get people's attention, and Manson knew exactly how. Take the first demo he gave me, for example. He didn't just hand it to me and say, "Hey, man, here you go. I hope you like it." Instead, he left it in a graveyard, for crying out loud!

But Manson wasn't just about shock—he was smart and intentional about using gimmicks as marketing, more so than most bands back then. Before one Halloween show at a club called Reunion Room, Manson and I went to a grocery store and bought chicken feet to decorate the stage and packs of gizzards to stuff into a piñata. Midway through the set, he leaned on a menacing-looking cane and asked the crowd, "Do you want some candy, boys and girls?" while pointing to the piñata. Then he handed them the stick to smash it.

Knowing what was coming, I stepped off the dance floor as fans broke it open. Instead of candy, chunks of raw meat rained down. People were horrified, but some skinheads in the crowd stomped on the gizzards with their Doc Martens, turning the floor into a slippery, disgusting mess. It was outrageous! But people talked about it, the word spread, the buzz grew, and more people came to see what crazy thing would happen next.

I got to join in on many of these antics—and even helped plan some. Once, Manson and I hit every Christian bookstore in the area, buying their stock of Jesus action figures. We turned them into Charles Manson figures by drawing Xs on their foreheads. At the last store, a guy stared us down and asked, "Are y'all in a band or something?" Manson smirked, but I kept a straight face and said, "Yeah, we're in a Christian band called Satan on Fire."

The guy looked shocked and upset and demanded, "Why you wanna call it that?" I told him, "A lot of bands and kids think the devil is cool, so we're trying to remind them where Satan and his followers are headed—to hell." This seemed to calm him. "I like that," he said and asked when we were performing. I gave him the time and place for the next Manson show.

Afterward, I felt inspired to create a series of flyers using photos of local glam bands (rumor had it Miami Riots didn't appreciate this). I presented these bands as Satan on Fire and listed the dates of Manson's shows on the flyers. I handed them out to who I assumed to be the Christian kids. Manson took it even further— he recorded a Satan on Fire demo and even printed a T-shirt. Meanwhile, his real band and its growing mythos continued to gain traction.

About a year before Marilyn Manson broke out and left the South Florida music scene, I started spending less time with Brian and more with Brad—but that's a story for the next chapter. The last time I saw or spoke to Manson was at Peaches Records in Fort Lauderdale during a signing event for his first album in the summer of 1994. Brian spotted me in line, laughed, and personalized his autograph on an album for me. I told him I was just stopping by to say hi, so he handed the record to some unamused girl who bought it anyway. Somewhere out there is a *Portrait of an American Family* album with my name on it—sorry about that.

That whole period was wild and a lot of fun, but it also made me reflect. I had watched and even helped someone who was focused and driven achieve incredible success. Yet, when it came to my own life, I lacked purpose or ambition. With no real direction or dreams to channel my energy into, I drifted aimlessly and eventually spiraled downward.

Chapter 9—Drugs

"No war stories!" That's what they tell you at a 12-Step meeting if you cross the line of sharing about yourself and your experiences and move into reliving or reveling in your experiences with whichever demons of addiction you wrestled with. You want to let people know you were there, but you don't want to take them back there. I remember this as I write this chapter, and I hope I have struck a balance.

I knew better than to do drugs. I had seen the after-school specials, read *Go Ask Alice*, heard Nancy Reagan's famous "Just Say No," and read the lyrics to Metallica's "Master of Puppets." I'd even watched my own family fall apart from substance abuse, so I swore I'd never touch that stuff. Drugs were for fools, and I wasn't one. But sometimes, knowing isn't enough.

Without getting into all the gory details, I will share my drug journey, which took a typical path starting with lighter drugs and low frequency before progressing in every way. A person who has never had issues with drugs is often baffled by this. Taking drugs is stupid. The downside risks to your health, family, well-being, and life far outweigh whatever short-term euphoria you might experience. That is objectively correct, but what one might not have considered is that pain avoidance is perhaps an even more powerful attraction than pleasure-seeking and motivation that might drive someone to take far more risks to achieve it.

A friend who recently overcame a long battle with alcoholism asked me if I had ever considered why I was so afraid to sober up and stay clean. I'm not sure I would have voiced it this way at the time, but looking back the fear wasn't so much about the initial uncomfortable detox experience; it was the fear of having to directly face all the problems from which I sought escape in drugs and the new issues I had created through drug abuse. I knew it wasn't wise, but I also lacked the tools to help me navigate through the turmoil of life, so I continued slowly down the path. Eventually, a drug brought me to a crisis point.

My aforementioned former criminal mentor, Freddy, was the first to get me to try a beer. At age 9, I was a total lightweight, and I woke the next day with my first hangover. Over the years, I played around with alcohol occasionally, but it never became a major issue (apart from the hospital episode).

The first time I crossed over from alcohol to drugs was when I was 11 or 12. My friend Scott's mom (and later his stepdad) didn't set many rules. His house was the go-to spot for everything you couldn't do at home or anywhere else. He had a stack of *Playboy* and *Penthouse* magazines he didn't even bother to hide, and his mom didn't seem to care that he smoked pot.

At first, I wasn't interested in smoking weed and refused it every time Scott offered. But one day, he got me high with secondhand smoke, so I figured, why not? It was fun and caused no problems—not at first.

By the time I was 15, weed hadn't made my life fall apart, so I thought everything I'd been told about drugs was just propaganda. I figured I'd be fine if I avoided the hard stuff. After a bad acid trip, which had convinced me I would either die or go permanently insane, I decided to pump the brakes on drugs altogether.

But after a year or two, I started dabbling again. What caught my interest during that time, though, were pills. The right ones could numb whatever needed numbing. I liked opioids the most; they did the job—until they didn't, and I needed something stronger.

I'd been diving into heroin culture long before trying it. I devoured everything by William S. Burroughs, watched *Drugstore Cowboy* on repeat, and idolized rock stars who sang about their love-hate relationship with dope. Even with all the cautionary tales, I still decided to go along with my friend Brad (Gidget Gein of Marilyn Manson) to visit his connection in West Palm Beach so I could try heroin for the first time. The warm rush that poured over me was immediate and more intense than I'd ever imagined. I had found the ultimate escape.

Drugs, like any sin, are fun at first; otherwise, you wouldn't do them. I enjoyed the initial thrill of getting high with my local rock star friend, Brad. The early days were full of wild stories—like when we rolled into Opa Locka (commonly called Dopa Locka) in Miami to visit our pharmaceutical distributors. While waiting at a red light, a group of sharply dressed African-American Muslims approached our car, selling magazines to raise funds. Brad asked what the money was for, and they replied, "We're trying to get drugs out of the Black community." Without missing a beat, Brad said, "Oh, we're going to do that right now." I was immensely relieved when the light turned green, and I could speed off before they responded. But it wasn't all fun and games.

Other times, things turned far more dangerous. One day, Marilyn Manson was rehearsing in South Beach, and I came to hang out. Brad and I took a bus to Liberty City, another well-known drug spot, to score. When we got off the bus, we tried to figure out which direction to head, and an older man approached us. His tired face, kind eyes, and the wisdom in his expression were impossible to ignore. Taking in our multicolored hair, pale skin, and overall out-of-place look, he said, "You don't belong here. It's not safe for you. Right over here is another bus stop, and the bus will arrive in about two minutes. You need to get on that bus and get out of here." Convinced he was our guardian angel, we followed his advice and left empty-handed but alive. Who knows what might have happened if we hadn't listened to him?

Addiction doesn't happen overnight. At first, you think you're in control. You convince yourself you can manage it, building layers of excuses and justifications. Then, one day, you wake up to the harsh truth: You're hooked, and you've been fooling yourself all along.

I started using heroin regularly on weekends with Brad and others in our circle. Soon, "weekend only" became the occasional weekday exception: *It's been a stressful day; I want to celebrate; I'm bored.* Those "exceptions" became more frequent until I used heroin not just with friends but also with strangers—and eventually, alone.

By 21, I had burned through my savings and started racking up credit card debt to feed my habit. I dropped out of Broward Community College, where I'd gone from a 4.0 GPA and making the Dean's List one semester to failing out the next. Desperation led me to sell everything I owned of value, including my $10,000+ comic collection, for mere hundreds of dollars to buy more drugs.

It got worse. I pawned cherished items, including my father's gold pocket watch, which had once been deeply meaningful. My reckless choices put me in dangerous places and situations. I was threatened, beaten, and robbed more than once. The pain and shame mounted, but by then, I felt trapped in a downward spiral I couldn't escape.

Drugs were a terrible form of self-medication I used to cope with my problems. While they offered a temporary escape from thinking about my issues, those problems didn't disappear—they grew exponentially as I sank further into self-destruction.

Eventually, I realized I needed help to get off this roller coaster, but nothing seemed to work. I took Methadone daily, but the clinic was in a drug-ridden neighborhood where dealers called out to me as I went in, "Got them pills!" Brad and I even went to a few 12-Step meetings, but we got kicked out of one for showing up high.

My grandmother, who had become an addiction counselor working in jails in Connecticut, flew me up north, offering me an escape route. Unfortunately, heroin in the Northeast was even more potent and plentiful. I even bought drugs at a Narcotics Anonymous meeting. Finding new people and places to fuel my old patterns didn't take long.

She even brought me to the jail where she worked for a day. In her mind, if I was given a window into what my future might look like if I continued down my path of destruction, I would perhaps wake up. When she told me about our day trip, I had imagined that when I got there, the inmates would sit me in a chair and encircle me as they blew cigarette smoke in my face, yelled at me, threatened me, and hit me a little to enhance the experience. To my surprise, the guys were fun and funny, and we talked, laughed, and played cards. My grandmother's plan didn't quite work, but it was still an enlightening experience. The inmates and addicts whom many look down on and think poorly of are often remarkable people with many gifts and talents to offer the world if they could only shake their demons and escape their various prisons.

I tried everything to stop—acupuncture, meetings, sheer willpower, self-help books—but nothing seemed to break the chains of addiction. I made multiple trips to detox centers, enduring the flu-like agony of withdrawal while telling myself, *This is it. This is the time I'll quit.* I remember going through withdrawals while staring down at the foam detox slippers with happy faces imprinted on them; they felt like mockery, flipping me off in my lowest moments.

I also went through 28-day residential inpatient programs several times. Each stint gave me some clean time and renewed hope that I'd find the key to sobriety. But despite my best intentions and all the promises I made to myself and my family, it never took long for "just one more" to pull me back into the savage current of addiction.

I was desperate, broken, and couldn't see a way out.

Chapter 10—Jail

I met Ali at a nightclub called Squeeze in Fort Lauderdale, one of my regular hangouts. She had just moved down from up north and was looking to score some heroin. We decided to head down to Miami, pick up the stuff, and return to my mom's place in Hollywood to use it since she wasn't home.

One of the many dangers of buying drugs off the street is the sheer uncertainty of what you're getting. You're placing a lot of unearned trust in the seller. Some drugs come branded from the source, but even that can be faked. You never really know if what you're buying is real, what it's been cut with, how often it's been stepped on, or its purity and potency. That night, we got some unusually strong stuff. It hit me hard, sitting me down right after I used it. But for Ali, it was much worse—it took her out completely.

In an instant, Ali dropped to the floor. I checked for breathing, but it didn't look good. Her lips were turning blue as panic gripped me. *Is she going to die? Am I going to prison?*

I quickly realized I needed to prioritize her life over my fear of consequences. I called 911 and reported the emergency, then scrambled to hide the remaining drugs and paraphernalia while waiting for the medics and police. All I could do was hope they would get there in time to save her.

Soon, the quiet of my mom's 55+ community was shattered by the flashing lights and sirens of emergency vehicles. First responders charged through the front door, giving the neighbors quite the spectacle. The medics immediately went to work on Ali, and thankfully, they revived her with Narcan.

Unfortunately for me, in her vulnerable state, Ali told the police everything. They searched the house, found what they needed, and arrested me for felony possession of heroin. Moments later, Ali was being taken away in an ambulance while I was led out in handcuffs and placed in the backseat of a police car.

As I waited in the holding cell, I saw two kids who were the spitting image of Beavis and Butthead brought in for trespassing. My heart was sinking, but I got a moment of comic relief when the officers, noticing the resemblance too, started doing Beavis and Butthead laugh impressions as they booked the nuisance pair.

When the detectives came to interrogate me, they used all the standard tactics you'd recognize from police shows. I had seen enough of those to know the drill. My grandmother, familiar with this world, had warned me over the phone, *"Don't rat, Billy."* When they pressed for where I got the drugs I stuck to my story, telling them, "I don't know. Just some guys off the streets."

"Yeah, sure," they retorted in visible disbelief. "You just got it from the Nigs, huh?" Their casual racism shocked me, and for a moment, I wondered if they realized how ironic it was for them to call me the bad guy in that room.

To my mother's credit, she stayed firm and refused to bail me out unless I agreed to enter a Christian halfway house she had found called Calvary House. After a couple of days, I reluctantly agreed. I moved into the house, attended church with everyone, and went through the motions, but I wasn't there for the right reasons. Nothing changed.

When it came time for sentencing, I was placed in a drug court program. Instead of jail time, I had to report for probation, drug tests, meetings, and even acupuncture. Apparently, I just needed to use needles "the right way" to fix my life. The program offered a major incentive: If I completed it, my record would be sealed, and I could move on as though none of this had ever happened.

But I couldn't stay clean. I lacked the motivation and vision to build a better life, so I kept returning to the only thing that brought me fleeting moments of peace, even as it demanded greater sacrifices. Eventually, I violated my probation with a dirty drug test and was sentenced to jail for an undetermined amount of time.

Jail was a harsh wake-up call. Time crawled—slower than the worst traffic jam. I had almost no control over my day-to-day life, where I went, what I ate, or what I did. The corrections officers were a mixed bag. One young African American woman joked about how handsome I was while taking my mug shot. At the same time, an older white guard called me out as a liar in front of everyone when I honestly mentioned my academic achievements.

The inmates were a chaotic mix of terrible and terrific, often in the same person. One day, I saw a man beaten savagely for speaking too loudly in another man's space. It taught me how quickly violence could erupt in that volatile environment. I kept my head down—except for when I woke up early, grabbed a Sunday edition of the *Sun-Sentinel*, and drew Gene Simmons' makeup over a photo of Al Sharpton. Hours later, an angry guy marched around, holding up the newspaper and demanding, *"Who did this?"* I played dumb and realized my sense of humor wasn't well-suited here.

Thankfully, there were safer distractions: honing my Spades skills, devouring books, and watching inmates react to TV shows. The highlight was when *Cops* came on, and everyone gathered around the screen. Without fail, when a suspect was caught after a chase, someone would say, *"I would have got away if that was me."* The irony wasn't lost on me.

After two grueling months, Judge Fogan reinstated my probation and gave me another chance. But as soon as I was released, I returned to using. A friend picked me up, and we headed straight to score.

Jail was one thing—I survived without being assaulted—but prison was another beast entirely, and I feared it deeply. Still, I kept playing a dangerous game. Once, while delivering pizzas completely high, I got pulled over. The officer talked to me briefly before getting another call and letting me go. Another time, a young Seminole police officer pulled me over. When he asked about my record, I convinced him I was reformed. He said, "Man, I always wanted to get a heroin bust." We laughed, and I said, "Feel free to search the car." "No," he said. "I believe you." Little did he know, a quick search of my back seat would have landed him the heroin bust he dreamed of—and a cocaine bonus.

Luck seemed to be on my side, but it couldn't last. I violated the terms of drug court again and went on the run, moving from one rented room to another as my life spiraled further out of control. Eventually, my reckless behavior caught up to me. A roommate discovered that her boyfriend and I had been stealing her CDs to sell for drugs.

She should have called the police, but instead, she gave me an ultimatum: get help immediately, or she'd report me. With nowhere else to turn and the weight of the law on my back, I made the call. Calvary House agreed to take me in once more.

And so, battered, broken, and confused, I found myself in their arms, ready—or maybe just desperate—to try again.

Chapter 11—Breakthrough

After another stint in detox, I returned to Calvary House. By this time, it had expanded from a single home into multiple quad apartment buildings. My plan was simple: lay low, let some of the heat on me dissipate, recoup, endure the "Jesus stuff," and plot my next steps. However, I was still trying to play the system, sneaking around to smoke (I only smoked cigarettes for less than a year, but it gave me something to do) and using drugs whenever the opportunity arose. Unfortunately for my plans, God and Paul kept getting in the way.

Paul Whetstone, the Director of Calvary House, was a classic redneck—and I mean that as a description, not an insult. He had a thick Southern accent and a high-pitched voice, which he used sparingly, only speaking when necessary. I can still hear him draw out the word "Weeeeeeellllll," stretching out as if giving himself time to consider whatever came after.

Paul, his wife Joy, and their kids lived their lives in the middle of this chaotic ministry, surrounded by dozens of struggling addicts like me. They aimed to show us the hope and healing they believed could only come through Jesus Christ. Paul's vision for Calvary House started small— in a trailer— before growing into a house with the support of Calvary Chapel Fort

Lauderdale. Eventually, it expanded into a cluster of buildings in a poorer neighborhood rife with drugs and illicit activity.

Places like Calvary House tend to be in the hoods or the woods because no one else typically wants that mess in their backyard. Paul lived modestly, investing his life and limited resources into this mission, even as most of us —myself included—were far from grateful and fought him every step of the way.

Paul was resourceful and made do with what he had. During my first month in Phase 1 of the ministry, when we weren't allowed to work outside jobs, feeding us all was a challenge. So, he grabbed whatever was left in the fridge and cupboards—corned beef hash, ketchup, and other random ingredients—dumped it all together, cooked it up, and served it to us with a wink and a smile. "Heavenly Hash!" he said.

Many of the guys lacked the life skills and discipline most people develop during their formative years. Paul worked to address this with clear rules, expectations of participation, and consequences for failing to obey the house guidelines. Alongside this structure, he sought to provide us with the wisdom and counsel we desperately needed.

"I know you get flustrated," he'd say, or, "Sometimes you get a Pacific idea in your head." At first, I dismissed anything he said after phrases like these, assuming his flawed English reflected a lack of intelligence. Over time, I realized just how much wisdom

Paul had to offer—if only I could set aside my arrogance and inflated sense of understanding.

I often tried to challenge Paul, engaging him in debates and bombarding him with theological questions I thought he couldn't answer. He never took the bait. Instead, he'd hand me a stack of books: *Mere Christianity, More Than a Carpenter, Evidence that Demands a Verdict,* and others. "Here you go, boy; read these," he'd say, shifting the responsibility back onto me.

Paul also had a knack for calling me out on my nonsense, holding up a mirror to behaviors I needed to confront. His approach wasn't always diplomatic, but it was effective.

One day, my mom came to pick me up for a reprieve visit where I'd go to spend the day at her house, and Paul said to me in his uniquely colorful, non-diplomatic way, "Boy, when are you gonna stop sucking on your Mama's titty?" If that statement offended you, imagine the anger that filled my chest as I stewed on his words. Paul's language was crass, but his point was spot on—I needed to stop relying on my mom to prop me up, grow up, and learn to be a man. Some guys thought Paul was too strict, especially with his zero-relapse policy, but in an environment like Calvary House, I came to see why it was necessary. I managed to get kicked out of the program three times. Yet each time, Paul graciously welcomed me back, investing even more effort into this hardheaded, difficult case, who often made his job harder than it needed to be.

Despite my resistance, breakthrough moments began to chip away at my defenses, allowing faint cracks of light to seep in. One day, a volunteer named John, who lived on-site and often drove me crazy, shared a verse to try to inspire me: *"Now to him who is able to do immeasurably more than all we ask or imagine, according to his power that is at work within us"* (Ephesians 3:20, NIV). I couldn't resist deflecting with my wisecrack Han Solo retort, "I can imagine quite a bit." But I didn't let on that for the first time in a while, I felt the faintest glimmer of hope. Another volunteer, Rick, patiently worked to help me see that hope was possible, even in my messy circumstances. One day, he asked me to stand and press my face against a painting on the wall. He asked me what I saw. "Dots, Rick. I see dots." He told me to step back a few feet and try again. "It's a painting of a ship that seems to be leaving the harbor at night and headed off to an adventure at sea," I responded. "Yes!" he exclaimed, "That is exactly right. In your life, all you can see are dots because your face is pressed against your current circumstances and looks bleak. However, in time, if you trust God, someday you will back up and see that all these dark and difficult seasons, those dots, are part of a masterpiece God wants to create in your life." Mic drop moment for Rick.

As a Calvary House resident, I often stared out the window for entertainment. I would watch the colorful neighborhood that unfolded outside. There was the Watermelon Man, who didn't use a PA system but instead shouted out the window of his truck, painted with watermelons, in a deep, booming voice, "Watermelon Man! Watermelon Man is here!" Then there was the guy who pulled up to the apartment complex across the street in a shiny black sports car—maybe a Trans Am, though I can't be sure. With his windows down, he blasted Van Halen's "Mean Streets" and shouted the spoken part loud enough to be heard over the music: "Lord, strike that poor boy down!" I remember cheering in surprise, realizing that black people liked Van Halen, too.

One day, as I stared out the window, what seemed like just another ordinary moment became something much more— a defining moment of transformation. Light broke through the clouds and into the room, catching my eye. My gaze shifted briefly to the drug deals happening not far away. In that instant, I recognized the fork in the road before me. I could return to the dead-end life I saw before my eyes, or I could turn toward the light—a light that represented hope, faith, and the belief that God was real. That He could lead me to a path of redemption and away from the destruction of my past. I chose the light.

Sitting there at my desk, with the light shining in on me in early 1995, I wrote a poem very different from the dark, despairing verses of my later teenage years. This one, titled "A Time to Heal," was about hope and decision. It was aspirational and, according to my mom—who proudly shared it with all her friends—inspirational. I've included it at the end of this chapter so you can decide whether it's poignant or cheesy.

Somewhere along this timeline—whether before or after that day, I can't say—I surrendered my life to Jesus again. At the pastor's invitation, I walked up to the altar after the message to the thunderous applause of the church, but especially of my mom and her friends, who had prayed and hoped for this moment for so long.

I wish I could tell you I believed, in that instant, that God would heal me of all my issues, addictions, and brokenness—that He would do more than I could ever imagine in my life, that He would somehow make sense of all the "dots" in my life. But the truth is, I didn't fully believe it yet. At that moment, I could only follow the light, like a prodigal son returning to His Father's arms, trusting in His love and care. I guess that's why they call it faith.

A Time to Heal

Mistakes I've made
Made more than a few
Bad seeds I planted
Sprout and grew

From all love
I turned away
Dressed in hate
I made my way

The walls I made
Reached to the sky
And they grew
More high than I

At wits' end
I looked above
He reached down
To me, with love

A love beyond me
Makes me feel
And lets me know
It's time to heal

My heart so hard
Scarred and bruised
My soul on hold
My mind confused

I laughed because
I could not cry
I lived because
I would not die

A drowning man
Without a hope
As I sank
I saw a rope

I grabbed it tight
Despite my fears
He pulled me in
And dried my tears

A love beyond me
Makes me feel

And lets me know
It's time to heal

Now I have an
All new joy
I love to build
Not to destroy

I'm not the man
I used to be
My ears can hear
My eyes, they see

Chains that bound me
Break and fall
I stand free
And I stand tall

Then my knees bend
And I pray,
"Dear God,
Keep me one more day."

A love beyond me
Makes me feel
And lets me know
It's time to heal

Interlude

Some of my favorite movies are redemption stories, for example, *American History X*. It's dark, with shocking and disturbing moments that sometimes make it hard to watch. However, you continue, not to be voyeuristic, but because the hope of transformation pulls you in and awakens deep desires in your soul. Maybe you felt some of that so far in this book.

When I first reread what I wrote in Act I, I felt unpleasant things inside me. Sadness, emptiness, other feelings I couldn't quite identify, and a little regret to round it out. How did you feel? Not about my story, but about yours? It is impossible to journey through life unscathed, so without question, you carry your own set of pain, trauma, and scars. I imagine your story differs greatly from mine, but did walking through my brokenness dredge up some of your own? How did that make you feel? What did it stir inside of you? As uncomfortable as that might be, stay in it long enough to understand, describe, and write down some things.

Act III explores practices and tools for healing, growth, and transformation. Before we get there, however, I want to take you on a journey of redemption. In Act II, I walk you through the redemptive arc of my life—the difference God made, the healing I experienced, and the unbelievable but real blessings that flowed into my life.

As we go through Act II, I want you to keep your story in view. I recommend you keep two lists as you consider your redemptive arc. Call one list "Redemptive Moments" and record every area of your life in which your brokenness was eventually met with redemptive healing and transformation. Celebrate and treasure these meaningful peaks of your story. Name the second list "Redemptive Opportunities," and on this list, write down all the broken areas of your life in which you have yet to see healing, transformation, or redemption. These are important for us to know so we can regularly invite God's help in what we cannot do, even as we take the steps we can.

I have grouped Act II's chapters into themes, much like in Act I. In sharing my story, I hope to inspire you and awaken your desire. You need not bury your pain; block it out and settle for limping through life. God wants your story to be a redemption story, too! It might look different from mine or anyone else's, but it will be beautiful and worth sharing and celebrating.

Keep your lists handy, read on, and dare to consider, "What might the rest of your show look like?"

Chapter 12—Unfairly Judged

Many believe the misconception that trusting Jesus as your Savior immediately makes all your problems disappear and leaves you with a permanent smile, living happily ever after. In my experience, that isn't true. Yes, some things happen instantly. For example, you are no longer condemned for eternity. God forgives you and replaces your guilt and shame with grace and mercy. You instantly receive God's Spirit living within you and gain a new, regenerative nature. These are incredible, life-changing benefits that shouldn't be understated.

However, your old nature still exists, and learning, understanding and living out your new identity takes time and effort. As I discovered, the problems you had before deciding to follow Jesus don't vanish; they still need to be addressed. The significant difference is that you no longer have to face them alone. You can rely on God's wisdom, strength, and power rather than your own.

One major issue that weighed heavily on me and caused constant anxiety was my unresolved legal troubles. Finding Jesus was amazing, but I still feared who might find me and what would happen when they did. I knew I had to confront this head-on if I wanted to move forward in a lasting way.

While sorting through my life at the Calvary House, I decided to turn myself in. I told Paul, the Director, I was ready to face the consequences, no matter how much I dreaded them. I called the police department and learned that since I was in a program, I could remain there until my court date a few weeks later.

Unfortunately, my case was assigned to a new judge because the previous one was retiring. I had read about this new judge in the local newspaper. She was known for being tougher on drug crimes and had criticized Judge Fogan, the former drug court judge, for being too lenient. Fear gripped my throat in a chokehold. This was my second probation violation. For the first, I had served two months in jail. Would this judge sentence me to six months? Twelve months? Or even a year and a day, which would mean prison?

I had survived jail, but prison was a terrifying prospect. My fate was completely out of my hands. Despite my fear, I leaned into God for strength, trusting that my destiny ultimately rested in His hands. God took my tiny mustard seed of faith and moved a mountain for me.

To understand the miraculous nature of what happened next, you need to know how the phone system worked at Calvary House. Back then, none of us had cell phones, and most didn't even have pagers. There was a shared phone mounted on the outside wall of one building. Residents could use it to make or receive calls, but there was no answering machine. If someone called and we didn't pick up, the phone just rang until they gave up.

A guy ran down to my building one day and told me I had a phone call. I rushed over to answer it and immediately realized how fortunate I was. Unlike dozens of missed calls before, this one hadn't gone unanswered. On the line was a woman explaining that Judge Fogan was trying to clear his open cases before retiring. She asked if I could move my court appearance to that week. "Yes!" I blurted out, amazed this was happening. It didn't feel like luck. I knew I had made my mess and needed to face it directly, but it felt like God was not only with me in the mess but also tipping the scales slightly in my favor.

Excited, I told everyone what had just happened, and the guys celebrated with me. The fear lingered, but the night before my court date, I felt compelled to pray—not for myself, but for others. I briefly mentioned my situation but spent most of the time praying for the people and problems I knew about, hoping God would tip the scales for them, too. Surprisingly, I felt a deep peace and slept well that night.

I was grateful Paul was going with me to court. Knowing God is with you is comforting, but having someone who cares present during your trials—literal or figurative—adds another layer of support. As several cases were called ahead of mine, I sat nervously, steeling myself for what was to come. Finally, my name was called.

Judge Fogan read the charges and asked if I had anything to say. I apologized and admitted that everything he said was true. I explained that I was now clean, getting help at Calvary House (with the director by my side), and was determined to turn my life around. Then, the judge asked a surprising question: "Are you a Christian now?" "Yes sir, I am," I confirmed.

"I can tell; I see it in your eyes. You're not the same person standing before me," he said. He said it was time to move forward and put this behind me. He even checked to see if he could completely dismiss my charges, which would have erased my felony record. Unfortunately, he couldn't do that because I hadn't completed the terms of drug court. However, what he said next left me stunned.

"Son, it's time to put this behind you. Your case is now closed." I was speechless. However, the prosecutor jumped to his feet, demanding jail time. "No," the judge said firmly. "Then, at the very least, please reinstate his probation and make him finish that," the prosecutor insisted.

"No," Judge Fogan repeated. "Mr. LaMorey's case is now closed." He struck the gavel, ending all my legal troubles with one decisive action.

Because of procedural rules, I had to be taken in one more time for processing, which included a strip search and sitting in jail for about six hours. But after that, I was free. I never returned to jail—except as a visitor. Joy, amazement, gratitude, and disbelief flooded my mind as I tried to understand what had happened. If this were a movie scene, I wouldn't have believed it was realistic.

The prosecutor was right: What happened to me was incredibly unfair. By all accounts, I should have gone to jail or at least been required to complete the terms of my probation. Instead, I walked away scot-free, undeservedly. It was the same unfair judgment God shows anyone who places their trust in Him. Despite our guilt, He mercifully sets us free and gives us a fresh start.

As one pastor I know often said, "Life isn't fair. Hell is fair, and everything else is grace." Because of God's unfair grace, and Judge Fogan, I now had the chance to rebuild my broken life.

Chapter 13—Trust Me

When you lie, steal, manipulate, and live erratically, a crazy thing happens: People stop trusting you. Funny how that works. Some people won't care about your claims of change, but those who care about you might want to trust you again—though understandably, they'll hesitate because you've burned them before. This creates a challenging tension when you're trying to change. On one hand, you feel hurt that people don't trust you and may have set boundaries to protect themselves. On the other hand, you feel ashamed because, deep down, you know they're right to protect themselves after what you've done. You might also feel anger and resentment: *I said I'm sorry. I've changed. Can't we just move on?* If you've been on either side of a broken relationship—and you probably have—you know this tension all too well.

Trust is the currency of relationships; you can't get far without it. So what do you do when the trust account is empty? During my journey out of brokenness, I found a path to rebuilding trust—the trust we need and want but don't always deserve.

Since trust is like currency, let's stick with that metaphor and apply it to actual money. After an intense period of addiction—or any life implosion—you don't have one mess to clean up; you have many. The sheer amount of work ahead can feel overwhelming. That's why many people return to the self-destructive life they're trying to escape. It's easier to go back than to push forward with the slow, steady, and demanding repair work. But in life, you have to choose your pain. It's better to choose the pain of repair than the pain of despair.

One area I had to repair was my finances. My immediate problem? I didn't have any money to manage. My bigger problem? My credit was in shambles from years of irresponsibility. Creditors were constantly calling, trying to collect debts, all with interest piling on. Eventually, I connected with a local credit agency that helped negotiate fixed repayment amounts and consolidate my debts. This allowed me to pay one set amount each month, which they distributed to my creditors. I set aside money from my paycheck each week, and over a couple of years, I paid off everything. I was finally debt-free!

That day was a milestone for me, and I still keep the final receipt as a reminder of how far I've come. But even though I'd paid off my debt, who would trust me with money again after my track record? Slowly, I began rebuilding my financial reputation. I started with a prepaid credit card, making timely payments. Over time, I was approved for a small credit line, which eventually grew. As my credit history improved, so did my score. Today, my credit score is over 800—a far cry from where it once was. I'm not sharing this to impress you but to show how trust can be rebuilt. Just as creditors now trust me again, relational trust can also be restored.

My creditors didn't begin to trust me because I had stopped the destructive behavior that made me indebted, felt terrible, or even promised to repay them. Trust was rebuilt only after repaying my debt and demonstrating consistent, responsible behavior over time. The same is true with the people we love but have let down, hurt, or betrayed.

The first step to rebuilding trust is to stop the harmful behavior. Without that, nothing else matters. Next, you need raw honesty—with yourself and others. You can't excuse bad decisions or destructive behavior by pointing to your hardships. You must stop playing the victim and own that your actions hurt people, even if that wasn't the intention. This isn't easy to accept, but it's crucial for both personal growth and rebuilding relational trust.

Rebuilding trust also involves making amends. For me, that meant offering financial restitution when appropriate, genuine contrition, apologies, and making things right wherever. Trust, like debt, usually isn't repaired overnight. Bear this in mind so you don't get discouraged while trying to do the right thing. Just like it took time for me to repay my financial debt and come to an excellent credit score, it takes consistent, trustworthy behavior over a long time to restore what was lost.

I say all this now, but at the time, I felt all the hurt and frustration one does who is sincerely sorry about their wrongful behavior and wants to move forward but hasn't yet done the work to rebuild trust.

Over time, as I stopped my destructive behavior, practiced honesty, and consistently made responsible choices, people began to trust me again. Family, friends, employers, and even creditors lowered their guard. They entrusted me with responsibilities, resources, and even their secrets. Today, people trust me with things as personal as their spiritual growth—a humbling responsibility, given how untrustworthy I once was.

Trust, once broken, cannot be demanded. But it can often be rebuilt through a transformed life, demonstrated by consistent, responsible, and trustworthy behavior.

Chapter 14 — The Long Shot's Heroes

Sometimes, when people hear my story, they marvel and say, "Wow, you really turned your life around!" I always thank them, recognizing they're as amazed by the transformation as I am. But I also redirect the credit to God, who saved my life and changed my story forever.

At the same time, it's important to acknowledge that change requires a willing participant in God's redemptive work. God always works with people in His process of transformation. And it's not just the person being changed—God also uses a variety of people as agents of change along the journey. You need people who model the right way to live, encourage you, speak challenging truths you don't want to hear, and take personal risks to provide opportunities that reroute you from destruction to the path of life. It would be impossible to list everyone who has played these roles in my life, but a few examples can represent the many people God sent to intervene on my behalf.

My grandmother on my father's side was a tough woman who endured many difficulties and fought bravely through them all. Growing up, I was amazed by her ability to work several careers from home long before remote work was common. Earlier on, she ran an answering service from her living room. Later, she operated a printing press, filling her home with the distinct smells of ink and chemicals I can still smell. After her husband, my grandfather, died of cancer when I was about 2, she faced many challenges alone, including the loss of her son, my father. Despite everything, she always had a soft spot for me; I was her connection to her Billy, my dad.

Through it all, she still struggled with her vices and addictions like others in the family. She smoked her Benson & Hedges until the end, when lung cancer took her life. She also was an alcoholic who found solace in the liquid handcuffs of vodka and peach schnapps. My grandmother was no angel, and yet she was my angel. In her 50s, she packed up her car and her little Yorkie, moved to Colorado, and earned a degree in counseling. She returned home to help troubled souls as the head counselor in Addictions Services at Corrigan-Radgowski Correctional Center in Montville, Connecticut. When she learned of my struggles with heroin addiction, she flew me from Florida to Connecticut to give me a fresh start. Although I wasn't ready to accept help then, her advocacy was astounding. She worked tirelessly to get me into detox and then a 28-day residential program—not once, but twice. She let me live in her home, guided me to recovery resources, and even took me to her workplace at the jail, hoping to scare me straight.

When it became clear I hadn't changed and I wanted to return to Florida, she didn't give up on me. She regularly wrote letters and sent cards of encouragement when I was down and out. Never underestimate the impact of someone believing in you when you can't believe in yourself. My grandmother passed away in 1995, just before profound changes began in my life. While I wish she had lived to see her investment in me pay off, I'm profoundly grateful that this broken woman's love for her broken grandson made such a difference in God's redemptive plan.

My mother also played a critical role in my transformation. While discipline wasn't her strongest suit, she excelled at providing love, stability, and modeling hard work. There came a time when she had to make a decision contrary to her nature, but necessary to save my life. My mom kicked me out of her house. We've all heard of enablers—people who love someone stuck in destructive cycles but unknowingly help them stay trapped. My mother realized that letting me use drugs without consequences and providing a rent-free place to live was only making things worse. With the support of her church friends, she put all my belongings in storage, paid for one month's rent somewhere else, and told me I couldn't stay in her home anymore. While it felt like a betrayal to me then, it forced me to face reality. That difficult choice became a catalyst for change.

Though my mother asked me to leave her home, she never abandoned me. She learned to help in ways that didn't enable my behavior and constantly prayed for me. Never underestimate the power of a praying mom! Even in my darkest moments, she prayed faithfully and enlisted her friends and everyone else she could convince to pray for her wayward son. Years later, I'd meet people who said, "You know, I used to pray for you." Thank you to everyone who prayed for me—especially my mom. Through it all, she never stopped believing or praying, and I'm profoundly thankful and indebted. She should be called Saint Frances.

It wasn't just my family who helped me. Sometimes, God uses strangers who become friends. One was Tim Ravenna, a man my mom knew from church. He had a beautiful family and owned a successful marketing and graphic design company in Hollywood, Florida, and somehow made room in his life for an actively using drug addict with no marketable skills. Tim gave me a job at Ravenna Design, more out of my necessity than his.

I learned to organize, work on a Mac, clean up, and find ways to be helpful—a job that provided much-needed stability. It gave me an income for food and rent, responsibilities to keep me out of trouble, and time with normal people doing productive things.

The business being right near the train tracks provided some bizarre experiences and encounters with interesting people we still talk about to this day. There were regulars like the self-dubbed Moon Cricket, who kept busy with odd jobs while waiting for his breakout moment. And then there was the day that me, Tim, and Tim's son Noah fortuitously stood at the office doorway facing the train tracks at just the right time to watch a hobo jump off the train as it slowed, roll over, pop up like a Weeble Wobble, and walk over to us. When he asked for money, Tim wisely declined, instead offering the man some popcorn as it was the only food on-site. We were all shocked when our new friend refused, saying, "I can't … my teeth," and then, as if sensing we needed further explanation, popped out his bottom row of fake teeth with his tongue and rapidly sucked the device back into his mouth, smiling and bouncing off to his next adventure.

Tim also invited me into his family's life. We shared meals at his home and restaurants. His kids, Sara, Noah, and Monica, welcomed me and laughed at my stories. These experiences showed me how good life could be beyond addiction. Years later, it was an incredible honor when Sara asked me to officiate her wedding to Joey.

If you're struggling and feel no one has helped you, look again. Help may be there in ways you haven't recognized yet. Don't give up if you're trying to help someone and haven't seen the change you hoped for. Breakthroughs rarely happen on our timelines. As the 12-step community says, "Don't leave a minute before the miracle happens."

That's not just for the person in need; that's a reminder to those trying to help that person, too. I've lamented the people I didn't have in my life, like a father or siblings. But time has taught me to appreciate the people I have had. Celebrate the heroes God places in your life—those who take risks on the long shots and change lives forever.

Chapter 15—Identity

Who are you? At your core, when you strip away the noise and nonsense, what belief, behavior, or association most accurately defines who you are, why you exist, and how you live? Like many, as a kid, I defined myself by what I liked—*Star Wars*, Marvel, gaming, and the like. By my teens, my identity revolved around the music I listened to. That's why I felt so offended as a teenager when two girls a few years older than me, residents in a Christian drug rehab, said, "Bill, you're not a metalhead; that is not who you are." I no longer cared that they were pretty or that one of them knew the guys in Helloween; they became 50% less cool to me in a sentence. Their words struck my ego because my metal street cred was solid. But deeper, it unnerved me because it left me questioning, *If I'm not a metalhead, then who am I?* I pushed that question aside but had to confront it years later as I transitioned from one chapter of life to the next.

Though your appearance doesn't define you, it often sends strong signals about your identity. Over time, I realized there was a disconnect between how I looked and who I was becoming. One night, during my wilder days, I shaved my head. It shocked everyone around me. The change from long hair to bald was drastic, but my wardrobe still reflected my old identity. Eventually, I didn't feel comfortable in my usual attire—T-shirts featuring bands like the Dead Kennedys; or slogans like "Remember Kids, Satan Loves You" and "I Scream, You Scream, We All Scream for Heroin"; or even my beloved Doc Martens. They no longer aligned with the person I was growing into.

I decided to discard those clothes and start fresh. With help from my mom and the thrift store, I assembled a modest wardrobe: five dress shirts, two pairs of Dockers, and one pair of dress shoes. I wore them everywhere—work, church, and social events. Later, I added casual items like shorts and plain T-shirts, with a pair of sneakers to round out my attire, as dressing up for BBQs was uncomfortable and a little weird. Mercifully, my new group of friends and their girlfriends took pity on my minimalist fashion sense. One day, they took me to Old Navy, commandeered my credit card, and loaded a cart with stylish casual wear. Though I protested, they made the purchase, and I immediately felt better. Updating my wardrobe didn't just change my appearance—it helped me step more confidently into my evolving identity.

Environments also play a huge role in shaping and reinforcing identity. As I grew, I realized nightclubs and shooting galleries no longer fit the life I wanted. As a new Christian, church seemed the right place to be, but it was tough to feel like I belonged. The familiar places of my past still felt more comfortable than the new, unfamiliar ones.

I recently returned from a visit to Calvary Chapel Fort Lauderdale with Rebecca. I was delighted to see that Calvary House was proudly and prominently displayed as one of their redemptive ministries and even given celebration from the main stage. However, when I was in the Calvary House program, I struggled with shame and insecurity. Even though we had a relatable pastor at the time with a past similar to my own, Calvary House felt like the "red-headed stepchild" of the church's ministries. The guys in the program, myself included, were embarrassed to be associated with it. We'd ask the van driver to drop us off in the back lot to avoid attention. But sometimes, Ponch, a fellow resident and driver, would park at the front entrance, slide open the van door, and honk the horn. It felt like announcing, *The lepers are here!*

The truth is, I was projecting my shame onto the church. I assumed the "regular, pretty church people" had their lives together and didn't struggle with sin and issues like I did. Over time, I learned that wasn't true. A funny thing happens when you start attending church regularly. You realize everyone has their mess to deal with, even though some are better at concealing it than others. The more I attended church, the more I realized that the problem wasn't with them—it was with me. I needed to stop projecting my insecurities and embrace who I was becoming.

Many people never take the time to consider their identity deeply. Instead, they settle for surface-level definitions based on hobbies, political affiliations, or demographics like ethnicity, gender, and age. Others define themselves by their career, successes, failures, or traumas. While these aspects may shape us, they don't reflect the core of who we are.

For me, the most meaningful identity I've ever known isn't rooted in myself but in who I am because of Jesus and the work He has done for me. I've found a new identity by placing my faith in His death, resurrection, ascendance, and promise of return. Jesus redeemed my past, offering me the forgiveness I didn't deserve instead of guilt and shame. He is refining me in the present through His Spirit, and He has promised me a glorious future free from sin, disease, addiction, and pain in a brand-new body. (And maybe I will be tall—OK, I made up that part, but I hope it's true.)

The Bible offers countless truths about who we are in Christ. For example, Ephesians 1 says we are blessed, chosen, adopted, accepted, redeemed, forgiven, enlightened, included, and protected. These truths are powerful reminders of our worth. I encourage you to dive into Scripture, discover these truths for yourself, and write them down and display them where you'll see them often.

Every day, the old and new me battle over who defines me. The Bible acknowledges this struggle and guides to victory. More and more, I choose to discard my false selves and live out my true identity. I am a child of God, deeply flawed yet deeply loved and approved of. My life has a purpose, and one day, according to Jesus' promise, I will live forever in the presence of my good Father. This can be true for you, too.

Chapter 16—Friends

Whenever you leave one season of life and enter another, there's sometimes a relational consideration: Will or should your current friends continue with you as you step into new territory? This question might surface after a traumatic event like a divorce or even a happy event like winning the lottery. It's also something to consider when moving past bad habits or addiction.

A great example of this dynamic is the "crabs in a bucket" mentality. Allegedly if you put crabs in a bucket, and one tries to climb out, the others will pull it back down or tear it into pieces. The other crabs don't want to see that crab do better than them, so rather than following the motivated crab to freedom, they pull it back so they can all be doomed together. This idea was first introduced to me by my friend Brad (from Marilyn Manson) while we were using drugs. People don't usually intend to pull you back into the bucket, but it happens all the time. Cutting ties with most of my friends was an incredibly difficult decision, but essential to giving myself a real shot at change.

It works both ways, though. When you embrace faith, like becoming a "Jesus freak," some of your old friends may find you insufferable—not because you preach at them, but because of how you live and what you believe. For example, after being clean and following Jesus for a while, I decided to head back to the nightclub Squeeze one night to see what would happen. I ran into Brad, who said, "I heard you found Jesus." Before I could respond, he finished his joke, "I didn't know He was lost." Good one.

Letting go of old friends wasn't easy; I became very lonely. I loved attending church and spending time with my mom, but I didn't love the idea of my mother being my only social outlet. (Love you, Mom!) Thankfully, she introduced me to Kevin and his family. Kevin, his sister Nanette, and their parents welcomed me into their home for cards, board games, ice cream and fellowship like I was part of the family. Finally, I began building relationships again.

Around this time, I moved out of Calvary House and rented a room. The homeowner's son, Mike, was also a recovering addict, and we started attending church together. Shortly after, in a desire to learn more, I enrolled in a Bible college extension campus at Calvary Chapel Fort Lauderdale. Sometimes, the smallest steps have significant consequences. This one became vocationally important later but immediately impacted my relationships.

After class one day, I met Bob and Jason. They seemed cool, and as we talked, I learned they had until recently been in a Christian hardcore band called Strongarm, which had done well in that scene. Digging deeper, I discovered Bob had been in a local heavy metal band called Amboogalard, where his friend Jeordie had played before replacing Brad in Marilyn Manson. We realized we'd briefly met years earlier—Bob with his purple mohawk and me with my long blue hair. How could we not be friends?

Hanging out with Bob and Jason helped me relearn how to have fun without doing drugs. We watched the Florida Panthers, devoured too many chicken wings, and played Spades, complete with my next-level smack talk. Our friendship and faith grew, creating a supportive circle that remains strong to this day, even if it is now limited to getting worked up together over current events and doing deep dives on heavy metal in a text thread many miles apart.

Eventually, I reconnected with old friends who weren't part of my addiction, like Greg, Rich, and Stew. My high school friend Stew had moved to Missouri but invited me to visit. In St. Louis, I met his wife Angie, and we spent time exploring Six Flags, the Arch, frozen custard and the uniquely bad pizza Missouri is famous for. I shared how my faith in Jesus had transformed my life, and to my amazement, they were both incredibly receptive. They even committed their lives to Jesus. It was an incredible feeling to positively influence my friends after years of being a bad one. When Stew and Angie moved back to Florida, they joined my church circle and became part of my new community of friends.

Not all stories had happy endings. I knew Meg from the Marilyn Manson days. She really liked me, which resulted in her also becoming a heroin user. I had introduced her to the drug after she begged me to try it. As I was finally beginning to thrive, grow in my faith, and build some new friends, I heard on the street that Meg had died of an overdose in her car behind the KFC in Opa Locka, near where we bought drugs. Desperately hoping this wasn't the case and hoping to disprove it, I called the Japanese restaurant she worked at and asked to speak with her. The girl who answered put me on hold, talked to someone else in the background, and came back with a shockingly expressionless and blunt answer that can sometimes accompany broken English, "Meg? She dead already." I hung up as my heart sank. I felt terrible for her and her parents. What a tragic thing to happen to a young woman in her early 20s. I felt immense guilt, knowing I'd played a role in her downfall.

I poured my grief into a journal, writing to God and committing to serve Him however I could. "I've spent my life working against you. I'm sorry. Please use me for whatever purposes you may have going forward. I'm at your command." I couldn't save Meg, but I refused to sit on the sidelines if I could help anyone else. I knew I couldn't atone for my past—that was Jesus' job—but I vowed to be an instrument for good moving forward and committed my life for His purposes.

Years later, I got to spend some time with Brad one more time after getting married. By then, we were opposites: He had long green and red dreads and rocker attire, while I had a church-boy haircut and square clothes. He came to a church service with my wife, Rebecca, and me and listened respectfully to the music, the message, taking it all in. He and I grabbed some dinner after I dropped off my wife. As he considered the church service and where I was then versus before, he told me, "Bill, I'm so happy for you. You look happy, your wife is beautiful, and you seem to have your life together. I wish I could have this, but it's not for me." I told him I'd pray for him and always be available to talk.

Brad eventually got clean and was excited about art showcases he was doing in Los Angeles, but one day, I got a call from our mutual friend Darla. Brad had relapsed and was found dead with a needle in his arm. Losing him was heartbreaking. Knowing my old friend with the million-dollar grin and worldwide dreams didn't get his happily ever after story. He was not the first or the last friend from back in the day to suffer such a fate. I often ask myself, "How am I the one who got away?" It's not a question with a satisfying answer, but wrestling with it helps me mourn the friends I lost and express gratitude for the divine intervention I didn't deserve.

The friends we choose matter deeply. Years ago, I heard Andy Stanley say, "Nothing will determine the quality and direction of your life more than the friends you choose." That quote has stuck with me; my wife and I often repeated it to our kids. It's true, running with lions beats staying in the bucket with crabs. Still, I hope to circle back and help some crabs escape, too.

Chapter 17—Work

I got my first job selling newspaper subscriptions to the *Hollywood Sun-Tattler* when I was 11. A surfer named Mark, with long, curly blonde hair, would drop me and other kids off in his van to go door-to-door selling subscriptions in the evenings. Was that legal? It was the '80s.

Throughout my teens, I worked at grocery stores, bootleg T-shirt print shops, a bookstore, telemarketing call centers, and other random places. I worked hard and always did well, except in anything related to food services (I'm terrible at that). Still, I had no clear vision for a career in case my childhood dreams of being a writer, comedian, or rock star didn't pan out.

Dropping out of college, acquiring a felony conviction, and living in a halfway house didn't leave me with many career paths. But through a connection at church, I got a lead on a customer service job at an import and wholesale company. Knowing my background could cost me the opportunity if discovered, I decided to be upfront with Bobby, the owner. I explained everything, hoping he'd take a chance on me. To my surprise, he did. Bobby admitted he wasn't perfect either and believed in second chances.

The company was staffed by a wonderfully bizarre group of people who constantly frustrated and entertained me. It felt like a sitcom waiting to happen—think *The Office*, but ahead of its time. Despite the hilarious chaos, I worked hard and earned promotions, moving from Customer Service Assistant Manager to Operations Manager. The four-and-a-half years I spent there gave me stability as my personal life improved and taught me skills I would later use in unexpected ways.

When I started taking Bible college classes, I didn't know how they would shape my future. Some of my classmates had clear goals: to be pastors, youth leaders, or missionaries. I didn't share that confidence. I was working full-time and taking part-time classes, but I didn't have a clear purpose. I just felt I was supposed to go deeper into Scripture, history, and theology. I had no idea how much this decision would influence my career and relationships—or how God was preparing me for a radically new direction.

Although I'd moved out of Calvary House within a year of working for Bobby, I stayed connected to the ministry that had transformed my life. Over time, I heard troubling reports. What was once a thriving program had devolved into "a flophouse with Bible studies." The founding director, Paul, had burned out and moved his family to rural Texas. His replacement's tenure ended suddenly and poorly. The most recent guy, who had recently graduated, died of a heroin overdose in the office bathroom.

By then, the ministry was on the brink of being shut down. When I heard about this, I felt called to step in. Through back channels, I expressed interest in becoming the director. Initially dismissed for being "too young," I eventually became a serious candidate. I was hired by Calvary Chapel Fort Lauderdale as the Director of Calvary House less than five years after graduating from the program. The inmates were now running the asylum!

One pastor warned me I had about a year to turn things around—or the property would be sold or repurposed. Challenge accepted! We assembled an ad hoc team committee and reimagined Calvary House as a "A Discipleship Ministry for Men." We revamped the structure, creating systems that provided residents with work opportunities at the church, discipleship by staff and members, life-skills training, and progressive levels of freedom and responsibility to prepare them for sustained success.

Working in recovery ministry was both rewarding and heartbreaking. Some days, we celebrated graduates who had rebuilt their lives and marriages. On other days, we mourned those who relapsed, were sentenced to prison, or died of overdoses. It was a roller coaster of emotions, but the highs made it worthwhile.

When I left three years later, Calvary House was thriving. Graduates succeeded, and the ministry had a steady stream of redemption stories. Today, it's stronger than ever. Every time I see their success stories, I'm amazed at how God used Calvary House to save my life—and later used me to save Calvary House.

It's a reminder that God can do anything. And that there was much still to come. "More than you can ask, think or imagine" indeed, Rick.

Chapter 18—Family

I will never forget her radiant smile and how the room brightened when she floated into the church auditorium with her friends. She was stunningly beautiful. For a brief moment, I let myself imagine what it would be like to date—or even marry—a girl like that. But, like a goalie defending a net, I quickly caught the thought and threw it away before it could settle.

"What business do I have even thinking about that? My life is a war-torn aftermath, and I have nothing to offer anyone except a lot of extra baggage. I live in a halfway house, don't have a career or even a car, and time will tell whether I return or not to the wayward living that put me in my current position." With such harsh self-talk, I bottled up the romantic fantasy and returned to my business. I kept hoping to catch another glimpse of her at church, but in a congregation with thousands of members and multiple services, I didn't see her again.

Years later, God had done a lot in my life. Most people couldn't believe the stories of my wild youth. I looked clean-cut, had a good job and a nice car, and even took Bible college classes. One Friday night, after class, my buddy Craig and I drove across the state to Peace River for a canoe trip with some singles from the church. We arrived at the campsite around midnight and tried to quietly weave through the girls' tent section to get to the guys' area.

As we moved in near silence, a voice called out from one of the tents: "Halt! Who goes there?" A sassy young lady was demanding answers. She gave us a hard time, and I told her to go back to sleep before she woke everyone up. With the skirmish settled, we found the guys' camp area, set up our tents, and got some rest.

The next morning, I discovered the sassy girl was breathtakingly gorgeous as I saw her crawling out of the tent. I spent the rest of the trip trying to impress her. I shared my bottled Starbucks coffee and packaged Craisins and even won the "most Altoids-in-your-mouth-at-one-time" contest. At the group dinner at Cracker Barrel, I got Rebecca's email address, which she wrote on a Sweet 'N Low packet (yes, I still have it).

From then on, I began pursuing her—and maybe stalking her a little. We started dating a couple of months later. My charm must have been irresistible, especially when I took her out and said, "By now, you must know I don't think you're chopped liver." Then, I called after the date to make sure she understood that this meant we were officially dating. Smooth, right?

A year later, I proposed to Rebecca on stage in front of a cruise ship audience with her family's help; eight months after that, we were married. Nearly 25 years later, I am constantly grateful for God's goodness in putting us together.

Scripture says a husband and wife should be "naked and unashamed" together, symbolizing deep intimacy. We've worked to practice that kind of vulnerability in our marriage. We complement each other well; I see the big picture, and she focuses on the details. I handle the letters; she takes care of the numbers. I lighten her up, and she tightens me up. Marriage hasn't always been easy, but God's grace has helped us work through challenges, and I'm confident I'm a better person because of Rebecca. Without her, I would never have been able to do the things in life God has allowed me to do or even become the person I am today. Rebecca says the same about me, which amazes me.

God also blessed us with three wonderful daughters. From the moment I held each of these precious girls as a newborn, I knew they were gifts from God. God had given us the privilege and responsibility to steward these three beautiful souls for a season. Growing up, I didn't have much father modeling, so I learned on the job. I always worked to provide for them, but I had to improve at being present for them as time passed. Looking back, I have some regrets and wish I had been a better example in certain areas. But I'm thankful that Rebecca and I gave them a stable family environment—something I never had. They never had to navigate the kind of abandonment I did. Even with our faults constantly on display, Rebecca and I were able to impart the roots and wings we desperately wanted for our girls to ground them and carry them forward throughout their lives.

My daughters have also blessed me in ways I never expected. Father's Day used to be a dark, lonely day for me, a reminder of the father I never had. Now, it's a joyful day filled with thoughtful gifts, hugs, and my favorite love language—food! Their smiles, affection, and loving words have encouraged me countless times and recentered me in God's goodness.

God didn't forget about my wonderful, faithful mother, either. Even as a rebellious, selfish teenager, I observed her sacrifices and her loneliness as a single mom. I occasionally saw her notice a couple walking as they held each other's hands, and I perceived a barely detectable sadness in her eyes. Some men were interested in pursuing her over the years, but having been through two failed marriages done her way, she was determined to trust God and wait for a marriage done His way. After nearly two decades of faithful singleness, through a church friend, she met Richard, a man who also had a past but was pursuing a redemptive path through Jesus. They married in a Christian ceremony, and I even had the honor of officiating their wedding with Rebecca serving as a bridesmaid! It was a beautiful wedding and the marriage is still going strong more than two decades later. We may not be your normal family, but I am ever grateful for the exchange of beauty for ashes from our Redeemer into our little tribe.

The Bible says, *"God sets the lonely in families, he leads out the prisoners with singing, but the rebellious live in a sun-scorched land"* (Psalm 68:6, NIV). I often reflect on and appreciate how God pulled me from the desert lands of rebellion and placed me in a family. My friends used to call me the Great Indoorsman because I hated going outside in the Florida heat. Yet somehow, I agreed to go on a canoe trip that even meant sleeping outside under the stars. Rebecca was scheduled to go on a similar trip to the exact location one week before, which got rained out, and decided to join our trip at the last minute.

Not only did we need to be arranged in place, we needed to be in a similar place in life because we were so different. She was the goodie-two-shoes cheerleader, and I was, well, you know by now. She jokes that if we had met in high school, we never would have dated. But God's timing and purposes are beyond our understanding. His hand was at work, orchestrating every detail to bring us to the right place and time. Oh, and in case you haven't figured it out yet—the girl who walked into church that day and the girl who sassed me from the tent are the same person.

Chapter 19—A Redemptive Mission

To prepare Rebecca and me for God's incredible mission, He first had to push us out of our comfort zone—what I called "the grid." Our lives revolved around a small, safe, familiar grid in Pompano/Fort Lauderdale, where we rarely ventured outside. Life was good there. We were content, enjoying our church and workplace, Calvary Chapel; our condo; and the close-knit community of friends within the grid. But before we could leave the state, God needed to lead us out of the county.

My friend Bob Franquiz offered me a job as his executive pastor at Calvary Chapel Miami Lakes (now Calvary Fellowship in Miramar), the church he had planted a few years earlier. I had recently graduated from the Calvary Chapel Bible Institute and had been ordained as a pastor, so I enthusiastically accepted the position. Saying goodbye was tough. The pastor I reported to told me on the way out how sad he was to see me go because the church had big plans for me. I appreciated those words and wished I had known that sooner, but I still felt God leading me forward.

Leaving a thriving megachurch with upward potential for a smaller, riskier startup was daunting but exciting. Calvary Fellowship had only a couple hundred people then, but it was gaining momentum. Working alongside friends and being stretched as a minister was an incredible experience! I had opportunities to teach, grow administratively, and learn valuable lessons in a younger, smaller church setting—lessons that proved invaluable for the future.

A beautiful pattern also emerged: God's redemptive work in my life. He kept returning me to places of brokenness and redeeming them with goodness. First, Calvary House, and now Miami—not far from the streets where I once copped drugs. I committed to two years at Calvary Fellowship, sensing that I might eventually plant a church. Sure enough, as my commitment neared its end, I felt God was leading me into another redemptive mission.

In late 2004, Rebecca and I took exploratory trips to Connecticut, my home state, to discern if God was calling us there to start a church. We identified five potential areas that lacked the kind of church we envisioned. It quickly became clear that West Hartford was where God was sending us. Adjacent to Hartford, the state capital, West Hartford was surrounded by universities and served as an influence hub for the region. It was a strategic spot that we sensed God was sending us to.

New England has long been called a "preacher's graveyard" because its post-modern, post-Christian culture often stifles spiritual vibrancy. Many churches had closed or dwindled to a handful of attendees. The beautiful brick and stone church buildings, once full of life, were now mostly empty on Sunday mornings. In this context, God gave us a vision from Ezekiel 37, which I encourage you to read.

The scene is right out of a zombie film but even more incredible! In the vision, the prophet Ezekiel looks over a valley of dry, scattered bones, and God asks, "Can these bones live again?" I imagined Ezekiel shrugging his shoulders as he responded to God, "Lord, only you know." Then God breathes life into the bones, causing them to reassemble, grow flesh, and come alive. God shared this image with Rebecca and me, saying, "This region is spiritually dead, but I am bringing new life here. I don't need you, but I invite you to join My work to revolutionize this area again." A revolution? We were in!

Excited by the vision, we returned to Florida, received confirmation about what God was doing from the people who knew us best, sold our home, and packed everything into a Penske truck. With our 18-month-old daughter, we embarked on this new adventure.

When stepping into a dream, enthusiasm often competes with doubts and fears. On our first day in Connecticut, reality set in. I had an "oh crap" moment, questioning the wisdom of moving 1,500 miles from the family and friends who loved us. We had little money, no building, and no congregation—only the vision God had placed in our hearts.

But God meets us in those moments. Shortly after we stopped by our new little apartment with the historical graveyard behind it, we headed to the grocery store to stock up. While shopping, we had a remarkable encounter. A woman approached me to talk about Jesus. When I told her I was a pastor starting a church, she asked pointedly, "But do you know Jesus?" I assured her I did. We talked briefly and then said goodbye, but something weird happened.

She followed me around the store, and at the checkout counter, she stood right behind me and said, "I don't know if you noticed, but I've been following you." Laughing, I replied, "Yes, I noticed." She continued, "God told me to buy your groceries today to encourage you in His plans." I joked about returning for steak before thanking her profusely and accepting this generous gift. Her generosity wasn't just about the food—it was confirmation that we were on the right path.

The next day, we visited Marilyn and her husband Les for burgers, forming a relationship that would later enrich our church family. That small act of kindness and connection reminded us that God provides in unexpected ways, encouraging us to keep moving forward in faith.

Most churches these days launch with a 12- to 18-month plan, significant capital, a launch team, and a comprehensive strategy. We didn't have any of that. Within four days of landing in Connecticut, I started working in sales at ADT to pay the bills. Two months later, we held our first church service in the basement of the Elmwood Community Center. A few churches and friends contributed to help us get started, and we poured a substantial amount of equity from selling our Florida home into the effort. Despite our shrinking savings, God always provided for our needs through my day job and a few miracles. After a year of this, at the encouragement and with the help of a friend named Luke, we raised outside support to cover my salary for two years. This allowed me to leave my sales job, focus fully on the ministry, spend more time with my family, and even take a weekly day off. It was a grind, but we loved it!

Starting from scratch meant dreaming of the big picture while handling every small detail until others caught the vision and joined the mission. For Rebecca, this meant managing back-end administration and serving as the Children's Ministry Director. For me, it meant writing and teaching messages, preparing video worship, maintaining the website, marketing (including a radio ad on a rock & roll station that stirred up some controversy on Christian blogs), and preparing and printing the bulletins. There were countless other things, like staying up late to label invitations for new movers in the community to visit the church.

Thankfully, we weren't entirely alone. From the beginning, John and Suzanne, along with Mike and Lisa, were there to help. God sent more people at just the right time. Chip, then a fresh-faced college kid, joined with his girlfriend, now wife, Amanda. Nicholas, a nervous chemistry professor convinced we might be a cult, eventually joined in leadership after his wife, Susan, persuaded him we probably weren't. Many others came and went through different seasons, and God blessed their hard work, bringing growth.

Seeing the church grow was exciting. We reached 60 people by the end of the first year, 120 by the second, and 250 by our third anniversary. At our peak, the church had more than 600 people in weekly attendance before settling at an average of 500–550. This put us in the 96th percentile of churches in the United States—a remarkable achievement, especially in New England. It was clear God was doing something extraordinary. If this sounds like bragging, please forgive me. None of this happened because we were particularly wise or talented. Our "plan" shouldn't have worked. Yes, we were called, committed, consistent, and hardworking, but only God could provide the favor and miracles essential to our church's story. While numbers quantify growth, the truly inspiring part was the people and their stories of transformation.

The people in our church were amazing. They weren't just members; they became our friends, family, and community. We celebrated and mourned together, intertwining our lives over the years. What I loved most about our church was its diversity. Initially, we were almost entirely white. Then, one day, several black families attended. A man commented on how he loved seeing diversity in our church, and I—just as surprised as he was—agreed! Over time, more Black, Asian, Hispanic, and international attendees joined. Eventually, we became a multicultural church, something we became proud of and known for in the community. A few cultural ingredients contributed to many different types of people calling our church home. We were fiercely apolitical, creating a space where Democrats and Republicans could coexist. We welcomed everyone from every age, ethnicity and background with phrases like "Come as you are" and "No perfect people allowed." We didn't attempt to manufacture diversity. God's grace made it happen, and we embraced and celebrated it.

Reflecting on what God accomplished through our church and its incredible people left me in awe. Who was I for anyone to call me their pastor? Who was I to pioneer a fantastic community of people who were coming to know and follow Jesus and follow him together? They knew me as Pastor Bill, but I knew me; I knew "the rest of the man's show." I knew myself, my backstory, my flaws, and my limitations all too well, and even shared much of this publicly. Yet, God's call was clear:

"Brothers and sisters, think of what you were when you were called. Not many of you were wise by human standards; not many were influential; not many were of noble birth. But God chose the foolish things of the world to shame the wise; God chose the weak things of the world to shame the strong" (1 Cor. 1:26–27, NIV).

To any fellow fools reading this, be encouraged. God can and will do extraordinary things through you if you follow His lead.

Chapter 20—Round Trip

I had big dreams for the church God invited us to start. We would get our building, launch new churches and campuses, and one day, I would pass the torch to a mentee I'd been preparing for the last three years to lead the church into a bright future. In 2020, I thought I had 15 years left for this to play out. Little did I know that by the following summer, I'd be celebrating my 50th birthday one night and driving a Penske truck the next morning, with Connecticut in my rearview mirror, moving my family and everything we own back to Florida, leaving the fate of our church and family uncertain.

The latter half of 2019 was particularly challenging as we dealt with a "staff infection" and internal division, including a small cabal plotting to push me out. After many sleepless nights, difficult conversations, and stressful conflicts, things seemed to settle as we entered the new year excited about our "2020 Vision" plan. However, the world had a different plan for everyone, and we were no exception. Already battle-fatigued from the previous year, our staff team had to navigate the ever-changing COVID pandemic and its restrictive efforts. "Two weeks to flatten the curve" became one of the longest and most challenging years most of us have ever lived through.

Everyone had to chart their course through this time, dealing with fear, isolation, angst, and more. Many pastors and leaders had to put their personal processing on hold while leading their communities through chaos. Add the racial tensions, demonstrations, and riots after George Floyd's death and the heated political vitriol in the Biden versus Trump election, and suddenly, everyone was angry at everyone. The pressure cooker blew the top off the world, and a stew of toxic junk spilled out, splashing all over everyone. How do you minister to a polarized society at a time like this?

People were angry over masks, vaccines, and discussions on race or politics and pastors were on the receiving end of much of their frustrations. There wasn't really a win, regardless of how thoughtful and nuanced our approach was. Exacerbating all this was our church meeting in a high school that kicked us out for a year during the pandemic. So we pushed our services online and traveled like nomads for the next year, doing our services outdoors in an AA baseball stadium and later in a theater in Downtown Hartford until we could get back to the high school.

When I felt stretched to my maximum limit, a personal crisis turned our church and family upside down. A few years after moving to Connecticut, we noticed a recurring pattern: Winters became increasingly difficult for Rebecca to endure. Her moods and personality would change noticeably during the long winter season, and then she would snap back to her usual self

111

when the warm sunshine of spring returned. Over time, we realized Rebecca suffered from Seasonal Affective Disorder (SAD). Just like any form of depression, SAD lives on a scale: mild, moderate, severe, or extreme. SAD eventually became so extreme for Rebecca that even the first cool breeze of fall, which is a delight to most people, caused great anxiety because it warned her that winter was coming. As her condition worsened, so did her sadness, mood swings and despair during the winter months.

Rebecca tried many remedies to manage SAD: prayer, fasting, prescription Vitamin D, suntan booths, medication, counseling and more, but nothing seemed to contain the harmful effect of a lack of regular UV light. Typically, Christmas festivities were enough to get her through the holiday season before she experienced her greatest difficulties in the first quarter of each year, but 2020 was different. The stress of 2020, along with the isolation of lockdowns, was difficult enough to manage. When the torment of SAD was added, it became too much, and Rebecca had a complete mental and emotional breakdown by early December.

I was so scared for my wife that I sent her, with our youngest daughter, to Florida for rest and recovery. When our other two daughters and I joined them a few weeks later, I was amazed to see that warm smile again sparkling across Rebecca's face. It was as if a dying, wilted plant had been replanted in fresh soil and favorable conditions and sprang back to vibrant life.

When Rebecca told me that in her struggle, she had considered a permanent solution to the problem for the first time, I was grateful she was alive and well, grieved to know how badly she had suffered, and determined to make an incredibly difficult decision for her health and well-being.

Rebecca had fought nobly for 16 years through SAD, but now that I knew how debilitating her condition had become, I knew I could no longer leave her in that struggle. I needed to move her back to Florida, where she could flourish in the Sunshine State. But this created a dilemma: How could I do this for my wife while caring for the church we started that was now nomadic, scattered, and unprepared to function without the founding pastor?

We came up with the idea of becoming one church in two locations. Churches do this all the time, but only in rare cases are the locations 1,200 miles apart! So, in the summer of 2021, our family moved back to Florida, this time to Sarasota. We built a launch team for 180 Life Church (rebranded from Calvary Fellowship) in Sarasota and eventually held our first few services. What became apparent almost immediately after we launched was that it simply wouldn't work. I couldn't lead the effort to rebuild our West Hartford church and start a new church in a different state simultaneously, regardless of how hard I worked or believed. So, we eventually made the excruciating decision to shut down the

Sarasota campus to focus solely on strengthening the church back in West Hartford.

Managing this decision meant I flew from Florida to Connecticut for two years to do the weekend services while remotely working from Zoom for the rest of the week. In late 2022/early 2023, our Board agreed it was time to find my replacement so the church could benefit from a pastor on the ground full-time once again, and I would no longer have to try to live in two worlds where I gave my all, but neither our church nor family ever seemed to get the best of me. By God's grace, we found the right person to take the lead pastor role for the church, and on September 17, 2023, I preached my final message and said goodbye to the church and community we deeply love and poured everything we had into for over 18-and-a-half years.

Rebecca and I planned to take a three-month sabbatical after our church responsibilities ended to rest, recover, explore, and dream about what God had next for us. A friend told me he thought God had a much longer sabbatical planned, and I think he was right. At the time of this writing, it's been over a year, and we still don't have total clarity. It took me a long time to realize that I needed time to name and grieve our losses. We lamented after saying goodbye to the church we started, the town we loved, our friends, our favorite home, and more. There were even things to let go of that shouldn't have been there, like an identity built on a vocation. Sorting through all the feelings and losses of the past and confronting the fears, uncertainty, and anxiety of the future took a lot of time.

Waiting can be brutal. I tried to speed up the process and briefly returned to ADT sales. Shortly into this stint, a bad car crash that totaled my beloved Challenger but spared my life shook me from my Jonah moment. It confirmed that God still had a purpose for my life and repositioned me back into actively waiting. In this season, God stirred up my passion for this book, for which I've had the title for nearly two decades. I have no idea what God will do with this book or our lives once it's written. I only know His story and mine are not yet complete.

I hope sharing my season of uncertainty and waiting provides some comfort as you wrestle with the fogginess of your future. In previous chapters, I shared completion points and redemptive circles with you. While they ended redemptively by God's grace, each twist and turn was uncertain, tested my faith, exposed weaknesses, and prepared me for future lessons. I do not yet know how this current chapter of my life will end. Daily, I still fight fear, frustration, discouragement, and disappointment, but I find hopeful victory when I consider what God has already done in my life. He hasn't brought me this far to let me down now. He is always faithful.

Even as we struggle to understand why God brought us back to Florida, He has done incredible things for which we are grateful. Our girls have adjusted well to being Florida girls, and the two who graduated high school enrolled in state universities. Rebecca and her health are doing great, and SAD is a thing of the past! As for me, I've had a lifelong dream to author a book, and here I am, trying my hand at this writing thing. We celebrate God's goodness and lean into belief, hope, curiosity and expectation as we eagerly anticipate "the rest of the man's show."

Interlude

In addition to leading Tesla, SpaceX, X, and Neuralink, Elon Musk finds time to troll on social media and become the top-ranked global player of Diablo 4. He's the richest man in the world and must be among the smartest, all politics aside. Therefore, I was fascinated to hear his thoughts on Jesus. Here's what he said: *"I believe in the teachings of Christ. I believe in the Christian principles. Love thy neighbor, turn the other cheek, which is very important to have forgiveness because if you don't, you have an endless cycle of retribution."*

While that was cool to hear and a good start, it's not enough. There's much more to the story. Believing in the principles of Jesus stops far short of what he offers and what you need from him. Jesus didn't come merely to teach you good morals; He came to save you!

I'm so thankful that Jesus came to save us all. But like Elon, many people, including Christians, don't go far enough regarding what Jesus left Heaven, came to the dangerous neighborhood called Earth, died, and rose again to offer you. Being saved, forgiven, reconciled to God, having a place in Heaven secured for you, and more; is all fantastic. However, many people, including Christians, miss that there is more. Much more. There is a saying in dealmaking, *"You never want to leave money on the table."* Don't settle for less than you could have had. Most people understand this, but regarding Jesus, many—dare I say most—of Jesus' followers leave money on the table. They settle for less. The analogy is imperfect because you don't negotiate with God. Jesus came on a rescue mission, and you either accept the help He offers or decide to look elsewhere. Yet the point remains that Jesus has more for you than most are aware of or tap into. You may leave things far more important than money on the table.

There is more to the Jesus story than Jesus saving you from Hell, and going to Heaven when you die where everything is perfect forever, as solid as that is. The good news is that when you understand and begin to more deeply access the things that Jesus offers you, it changes your story here and now. You've read my story, and I hope you've seen how the power and presence of Jesus can turn things around. Even if you haven't experienced anything as drastic as I have, there is a greater life of health, healing and wellness available to you too.

As we shift into this book's third act and second half, I want you to think of your story, where it's been, and then begin to dream or imagine the rest of your story and what that could be like if you broke free from a former or current chapter and experienced transformational change in your life.

In Act III, I offer healing and growth practices for transformation. Lessons from the road, if you will. The chapters are intentionally short though many of the chapter's themes could easily be developed into a book. If I bring up a theme that connects with you, grab a book on the topic or speak with a wise counselor about it to dig deeper. In some cases I have included recommendations. Some ideas may not resonate with you, but if even one helps you break through a barrier, this book served its purpose. You can read through the entire section or skip to a topic that interests you. Many of the practices I discuss are beneficial even if you're not a believer in Jesus, but they'll be more effective if you are. In chapter 39 I explain how to accept Jesus' generous offer of salvation. If you feel that is something you need, I encourage you to read it first. I pray that you won't leave anything God offers you on the table. May your journey from brokenness to redemption and transformation become remarkable and fulfill everything God desires for you.

Chapter 21—Process Regularly

"You're a dump truck." My counselor spoke those words as I unpacked how I had navigated through multiple crises. I tried to keep our church moving forward during the COVID-19 pandemic while dealing with a personal crisis, which lead to planning to move my family 1,200 miles away. I described feeling stressed and anxious, which didn't surprise him. He continued empathetically:

"It's like you've just kept moving forward no matter what has come your way without considering how you are feeling or how it has affected you. You haven't slowed down to inspect or deal with the personal impact from any of the challenges, disappointments, heartaches, heartbreaks, or even any of the breakthroughs that you've been experiencing. You keep pressing forward, and as you encounter each new thing, feeling, or emotion, you throw it in the back of your dump truck like an annoying obstacle, telling yourself, 'I'll deal with it later,' but you never do. And what you're feeling now is the reality that you can't keep this up forever because the weight of each new unprocessed thing tossed in the back is getting heavier and heavier; it's slowing you down, and eventually, you won't be able to move forward one more inch. I suggest you pull over now and at least see what you're carrying back there and then see what you can do to lighten your load."

Can you relate to this? Do you sometimes, or even often, feel sad, angry, fearful, disappointed, aggravated, out of motivation, slowed down, or numb without knowing why? This was me for most of my life; I rarely made time to process my inner world. My counselor was right; I am a dump truck. Or at least I operated like one for many years. I knew something wasn't right, maybe with a foggy inkling of what and why, but I didn't want to stop and deal with it when "progress" was still an option. So I chucked it in the back to deal with "some other day," but some other day never seemed to come. When you don't process and deal with the things you carry in your soul, they don't go away or even stay the same; they usually worsen, corrode, and become heavier and more toxic. Eventually, the cumulative weight of such a massive burden becomes too much for your heart and mind, and you find yourself broken down and stuck somewhere in an emergency lane on the highway of life.

In those moments, you'd think you'd be wise enough to slow down, and take the time to sift through the collected rubble in your life to assess how to deal with it and get moving again. However, it's easy to make a different decision, which worsens things. You turn to whatever offers you a reprieve or escape, even for a few precious moments where you can forget. That could be drugs, alcohol, sex, porn, chasing money, spending money, gambling, a new relationship, fantasy worlds, or many other things—even good things, as long as they distract you. You know where you turn in hard times. You also know that eventually, those things U-turn you back to your broken-down dump truck, now with even more garbage to carry than before.

It turns out my counselor was right. Pulling over and sorting through the junk you carry in life is a much better way to move further and faster, even if it requires uncomfortable pauses for deliberate introspection. To move at full speed or to feel deep health in your soul that enables you to flourish, you need to understand exactly what you feel (or numb) and what causes it.

David is a much revered, yet tragically flawed, character in the Bible who was a mighty warrior and a composer of deep, thoughtful poems dripping with emotion. Don't believe the lie that toughness and tenderness are mutually exclusive. In one half of one verse, David poses a thoughtful question important to emotional and mental well-being whether or not you believe the Bible: *"Why, my soul, are you downcast? Why so disturbed within me?"* (Ps. 42:5a, NIV). My counselor and David call for a comprehensive inventory of the soul to figure out what the hell is going on (yes, I mean it that way, too) in our inner worlds. If you've ever operated as a dump truck for a long season—or even for as long as you can remember—you will experience immediate health and ongoing benefits from the following exercise if you practice it regularly. Let's call it Emptying Your Dump Truck or Processing Your Inner World, if that sounds better to you.

Step 1: Look inside. Climb into the back of that dump truck and decide you won't get out until you figure out what's there to the best of your current ability. This is important because as you grow, future inspections might reveal things you couldn't discern in earlier self-examinations. Don't worry about that for now. The most significant first step is to pull over and stop throwing more stuff in the back of your soul until you figure out what you already haul with you everywhere. This step is simple but profound; you decide to no longer live in soul ambiguity but instead to pursue clarity even if it is difficult—which it undoubtedly is. Once you press inward, you're ready for the second step.

Step 2: Notice and name things. What do you see in the dump truck? What long-forgotten traumas and pains do you uncover as you dig through the piles of your collected life experiences and related emotions? It is hard not to look away when you encounter buried ghosts, but take a breath, say a prayer, and be brave as you continue this messy process. And as you go through, name everything. Name the experience, the pain, the event, the person, or whatever the cause or catalyst might be. Also, name what you feel—or what you felt until you buried it— and now only sense as faint, ghostly whispers deep within your soul. Let no unpleasant sights, sounds, smells, tastes, or sensations associated with each thing scare or discourage you; keep digging and naming.

Step 3: Write down your observations. It probably doesn't help to immediately deal with your discoveries as they're unearthed from your soul. This process is simply about taking an honest inventory. It's a necessary and helpful part of your health journey, and this step is about merely documenting. When my counselor gave me the dump truck analogy, I went online, found an outline of a dump truck, printed it out, and wrote everything down inside that image. I encourage you to do the same or draw your own and use it to inventory what's on the shelves, floors, closets, and in the dark corners of your soul. If that seems too silly, write it somewhere in your journal or wherever you prefer. As you go through this process, you may discover recurring themes and patterns, perhaps from different events, circumstances, and time frames. This is where you want to proceed to Step 4.

Step 4: Group like observations together. You still learn about yourself here, and in addition to organizing and decluttering your soul like Marie Kondo, you discover more about what goes on in your inner world. Perhaps when the process is complete, you'll find two or three unusually large piles that you believe contribute significantly to weighing down your soul. This is great information! Write these observations down and keep inventorying and organizing until you're finished.

Step 5: Resist the urge to deal with these things yet or try to "fix yourself" now. Keep digging and cataloging for now. You unpack and deal with these discoveries in later chapters, but for now, you just figure out and label what's there. Is it fear, shame, guilt, regret, sadness, disappointment, abandonment, neglect, abuse, embarrassment, failure, or something else? Whatever you discover, write it down without judgment or remedy, and put it in the appropriate pile.

If you're weary of feeling downcast and disturbed within your soul, it's time to do the hard work of self-examination in a way that helps you discover and name what goes on inside and makes you feel this way. Simply going through this exercise, even without solving anything yet, decompresses your soul, releasing immediate weight because at least you know what you're dealing with after completion. You have clearer next steps for your health journey, whatever they might be for you. This is a difficult thing to do.

You likely have as much desire to dive in and sort through your own dump trucks as you do to dive into a nasty-smelling physical dump truck. Do it anyway! It's worth it because your mental, emotional, and spiritual well-being are worth it. Fortunately, if you practice this regularly, maybe monthly, weekly, or even daily as needed, it gets much easier and faster to do. Don't wait until you're stalled out and can't go further. If you're already there, don't hit your escape button again; things will only worsen. Hop in the back and get to work so you can get back on the road—maybe even a brand-new road—with greater clarity and a little less weight.

Steps to Empty Your Dump Truck:

1. Look inside.

2. Notice and name things.

3. Write down your observations.

4. Group like observations together.

5. Resist the urge to deal with these things yet.

Chapter 22—Break the Curse

Pastor Geoff graciously invited me into his office, listened to my question, and gave me a thoughtful, insightful response I never forgot and often shared with others, now including you. When reading James 3, the immense power of words becomes strikingly clear. Words can determine your life direction, set your world on fire, have a corrupting effect on an entire person, poison people and relationships, and are wild and almost impossible to control. A forked-tongue dilemma confronts you in this passage about the words you speak, *"Out of the same mouth come praise and cursing. My brothers and sisters, this should not be"* (James 3:10, NIV).

You curse people God made and adores, yet you tell God how incredible He is and how much you love him, James tells us. Tell any father how awesome you think he is right after you insult his child, and see how well that goes over. My question to Geoff was related to cursing and blessing. What does it mean to live under a curse? Geoff explained that the concept is far more damaging than words like #%*@ that you might hear or say. He broke it down to me this way.

"Some people have grown up in a family environment in which they were covered with a cloud of blessing. They were affirmed, encouraged, and poured into. Their family told their child that they loved them, were for them, that they mattered and belonged. These words seeped deep into their souls,

forming a cloud of blessing over them that moves with them wherever they go in life. Others were born with a cloud of cursing over their lives. They were told how bad, stupid, or wrong they were. Their flaws were constantly pointed out; they were constantly criticized, put down, and even beaten down with words. Not only that, they also experienced the cursing of neglect as they never or rarely heard words like I love you, I believe in you, you matter, you belong, you can do it, I appreciate you, and I'm so glad God put you in our family. These curses, including those of neglect, seeped into their souls and formed a cloud of cursing over them that also moves with them wherever they go."

Way to keep it light, Geoff! His profound words give great insight into brokenness, redemption, and healing.

First, consider what forms the cloud that moves above you wherever you go:

- What is constantly reinforced about who you are that dramatically affects your perception of yourself and how you live?
- What words were spoken over you?
- Who spoke these words into your life, and what was their net impact?
- How did these words define you?
- How did they shape you?
- What words do you believe about yourself and tell yourself regularly?

- Which words became a self-fulfilling prophecy because you believe these things spoken over you to be the truth?
- Which words affected the person you are today?

You likely have a mixture of clouds covering you as you experienced blessings and curses throughout your life. Both have undoubtedly worked their way into the fiber of your being, but in most cases, one outweighs the other.

In my life, I grew up hearing many blessings spoken over me, especially from my mother, who was ever gracious, loving, and kind. And yet, I never heard words from my father that I needed to. I still long to hear the words, *"I'm proud of you, Son,"* from my dad, which I never heard him say. And my stepfather, other kids, classmates, and various people spoke biting, soul-crushing words. You shouldn't forget that you are often your harshest critic. Don't discount that you speak or reinforce curses over yourself, too. The devil also speaks words over you and, hint, he is the Father of Lies, so filter accordingly. The saying goes, *"Sticks and stones may break my bones, but words will never hurt me."* However, the saying is untrue, so carefully consider how the words spoken over you throughout your life brought health or brokenness to your soul.

God speaks words over you; do you know what they are? The fantastic news is that you can be an agent of great healing by helping to change the clouds that cover you, and even the clouds over the people around you, with God's help and your intentional effort.

First, let's deal with the cursing in your life. (No, I don't mean naughty words, though if you feel conviction about that, then maybe ease up on expletives.) Instead, I speak of addressing the curses spoken over your life that poisoned you, corrupted you, and set your soul on fire. Please take a piece of paper and write two columns titled Remove and Replace. In the Remove column, write down the curses spoken over you that you sense weigh you down and hold you back in life.

Remember that some negative things spoken over you are true, even if they were shared in unkind or unhelpful ways. Confess those things to God, ask for His help to change in that area, and then choose to no longer let that curse define you. Your goal here is to separate the words raining over you and defining you from careless words that need to be removed. The next column helps with that. In the Replace column, write down a word of blessing to replace the curse word in the previous column. For example, I defined myself as fatherless for many years. But the Bible teaches that God Himself is a father to the fatherless, so I had to learn to replace "fatherless" with "child of God."

For people who grew up not hearing "I love you" enough, maybe it's time to replace "unloved" or "unlovable" with "loved

131

by God." Perhaps you don't know a lot about Scripture or where to begin. I encourage you to embrace identity words from the end of Chapter 15 as life-giving blessing words to replace the curse words defining and debilitating you. These replacement words do not only redefine you but also serve as a filter when others speak curses over you. Never let words enter your soul unfiltered and unchallenged. You need not permit curses to penetrate your heart; you can instead filter them through what God says is true of you and reject their labeling and destructive power. This is a process, but through time and repetition, you learn to reject the words of cursing and to live under the cloud of blessing God always intended for you.

It is not enough to consider only your clouds; you must also consider the clouds you form over the people around you. In the 10th grade, I had to go to summer school because I skipped school too much, and my grades suffered accordingly. I wrote a book report on *The Martian Chronicles* by Ray Bradbury, which my teacher asked another teacher who had read it to grade. This teacher, Mrs. DeShong, not only gave me an A+ grade but also sought me out and told me I was brilliant, a fantastic writer, and belonged in Honors English. The power of her words lifted my spirits and helped me believe things about myself I never considered. Her words of blessing carried me into Honors English the next year and AP English the year after, where I earned all As.

Such is the power of speaking words of blessings over someone's life; it is a power that you, too, hold. You and I speak words into others' lives that shape, steer, reinforce, or tear down what they believe to be true about themselves. You should use this power graciously and intentionally. I didn't always do this, and I know I spoke damaging words over the lives of people I know and love, just as many spoke over mine. If you regret this as I do, your answer is to repent, which means to change the way you think, confess it to God, and ask for His help in speaking life over people. This doesn't mean you can never correct or criticize others, though even that should be done thoughtfully and gracefully.

A starting point in practicing blessing is to do no harm with your words. My friend, J-Bird, once handed me a piece of paper with "Proverbs 18:6" written on it. When I looked up the verse the threatening message was clear; I really should talk less. Maybe that's a good start, but growing requires more of us, and a different verse is instructive in this: *"Do not let any unwholesome talk come out of your mouths, but only what is helpful for building others up according to their needs, that it may benefit those who listen"* (Eph. 4:29, NIV). So, how can you move from doing no harm to building others up? Simply speak true affirmations into other people's lives.

I developed the habit of acting when a good thought about someone enters my mind. When I think something nice about someone, and it is appropriate, I tell that person what I'm thinking since they probably can't read my mind. Maybe that looks like a random text celebrating a good quality you see in them or thanking them for how they positively impacted your life. Perhaps you call out potential you see in them that they don't yet see in themselves. Maybe you tell them you love them, are grateful for them, and appreciate them.

Are you thinking of someone right now that you can practice this with? You have no idea how much your words of blessing might challenge someone's cloud of curses and change the trajectory of their life. I bet Mrs. DeShong didn't.

Steps to Break Curses:

1. Consider the clouds of blessing and cursing over your life.
2. List words to remove from your cloud.
3. List words to replace those words with.
4. Consider the clouds you form over others.
5. Practice building people up and speaking life over them.

Chapter 23—Play It to the End

"Don't stop there; play the tape to the end," I often told residents at the Calvary House when they struggled with impossible temptations. I then painted a fuller picture for them:

"Right now, you envision sitting on a sun-soaked beach with a gentle breeze whispering through your hair as you curl your toes into the soft, white sand and sip slowly on a perfectly crafted piña colada, complete with the cute mini-umbrella and the cherry on top. However, those days of enjoyment are over for you; you're re-creating a fantasy that can't exist in your future. Yes, other people may be free to enjoy this, but for you, as the 12-Step folks say, 'One is too many, and a thousand is never enough.' The only drink you can control is the first; after that, all bets are off. Who knows how many you'll have after that, how long you'll run for, and what damage you'll cause to yourself and everyone around you. You'll likely empty your meager savings account once again to fund your binge, you'll probably lose your job, erode the little trust you had rebuilt with your family and friends, and you'll destroy your peace and vibrant relational connection to God. You may rack up another DUI, or worse, you may kill yourself or someone else as a drunk driver. You could easily end up in a holding cell in jail or in a detox where they're pumping you with benzos as every cell in your body writhes in agony. I might even end up doing your funeral, which would make me and the people who love you incredibly sad."

That might sound extreme to you. But if you struggled with alcoholism or any addiction, then you know it isn't. Yes, I threw a little dramatic flair in when I shared this with the guys, but I had to use everything at my disposal to fight a powerful and destructive force—self-delusion.

Delusion works against you in moments of personal temptation to convince you that whatever you want to do is worth the pleasure you experience and to make you believe that little or no pain or consequence follows because of giving in. Maybe your temptation doesn't involve a drink or a drug. It might be in the pantry, on a website, in a brick-and-mortar or online store, on a betting slip, or anything else you habitually turn to when your triggers are tripped.

However your temptation manifests, playing the tape to the end is a highly effective tool to overcome it in the moment so you can later wrestle with the underlying factors. This is less of a practice and more of a tool to keep in your health toolbox to prepare for the next time temptation waltzes back into your life. But we will discuss something you can do today to sharpen your tool to be ready for use as needed.

Your brain is an amazing machine that always operates in the background, doing incredible things even though you are often unaware of what it is up to. While your mind is meant to work for your benefit, the improperly trained brain, or hijacked brain, can function as a powerful tool that deceives and even works against you. One way you can trick yourself with your thoughts is through selective edits. Consider a well-made documentary. The makers usually advance a specific narrative. They do this to great effect through tone, strategic music, and by including elements that support their agenda, and editing cuts that might undermine whatever they are pushing. And it works!

Your brain runs the same game as it presents temptation in the most compelling light possible. It edits out all the crap that might make you consider if you should go down that dimly lit path, which is why you have to learn to play the tapes to the end. It's like saying to the brain, *"Thanks for sharing that clip; I see you paused it, so I'm going to hit the play button, and we'll consider a bit more how this particular story would end."* This doesn't just apply to the bad habits that trip you up regularly; it could apply to a big one-time temptation that could end with catastrophic consequences. For example, you might feel stress and financial strain and decide to "borrow" a little money from your company. Play the tape more and consider where this could end. Do you get caught and embarrassed, and end up in even direr straits? Do you end up in jail or even prison serving time where you are locked up and now branded as a criminal? Or how about the person you have an obsessive attraction to who is not your spouse? In your mind, you probably replay the fantasy to fulfill your desires. Then, you stop, rewind, and play it over again from the beginning. Instead, play the tape to the end and consider what happens after the point of pleasure. Do the guilt and shame become overwhelming, and you maybe pick up an STD to go with it for good measure? Does your spouse discover your affair, and all the happily-ever-after dreams you once shared together as a family are replaced with divorce, joint custody, and a bag of regrets? Part of why you must play the tape in your mind to the end is to consider the bad things that might happen if you give in and the good things you might have to give up.

My friend John meticulously followed his savings plan to pay for the beautiful new-construction dream home being built for him and his family. His wife was a serious spender. (There is usually a saver and a spender in any relationship to keep things interesting.) Whenever his wife came to him proposing a luxurious vacation, a new vehicle, or whatever else she wished to spend money on, he walked her into the room where the rendering of their dream home hung on the wall. He said, *"Sure honey, which piece do you want to rip off our home? Should we pull out the windows, the pool, maybe the HVAC system, or how about doors; who needs those?"* It was a little theatrical, but it made the point.

Whenever you give in to temptation in the moment, you rip off a part of your future.

Think briefly of the story you want to see in your life:

- What type of person would you like to become?
- What would you like to achieve?

- What kind of relationships do you hope for, and how long would you like them to last?
- What type of body do you want to have?
- What do you sense is God's purpose for your life, and do you want to live that out?

Whatever your dreams are, write them down in words or create a picture. Maybe even hang them someplace where you can regularly see them. Then, the next time that temptation embeds itself in your skull with warped desire beckoning you like a siren's call, run over to the representation of your dream and ask yourself, *"Which part of my future am I willing to rip off the page to give in to this temptation, and is it worth it?"*

So the tool is to stop hitting the pause button, to refuse selective editing, and to play the tape in your mind to the end. The way to prepare yourself to use the tool effectively when you need it is to consider in advance the negative consequences that this action might have on your life goals. Clarify your dreams that you rip off pieces of if you gave into temptation. This process helps you with something valuable but sometimes frustrating—delayed gratification.

Temptations promise you an immediate payoff in the present; you can have it right now. However, resisting the strong compulsion for your future means waiting. Waiting is hard, and I have met no one who enjoys it. That's why you need reminders to keep you on track. This one is a regular go-to for me:

"Do not be deceived: God cannot be mocked. A man reaps what he sows. Whoever sows to please their flesh, from the flesh will reap destruction; whoever sows to please the Spirit, from the Spirit will reap eternal life. Let us not become weary in doing good, for at the proper time we will reap a harvest if we do not give up" (Gal. 6:7–9, NIV).

This passage confronts self-delusion. Don't be deceived or self-deluded. Each decision you make is like planting seeds. Nothing might happen now, but you reap the fruit of your choices. If you keep giving in to temptation and lesser desires, you one day reap a harvest of destruction. However, if you sow spiritual seeds, your harvest is eternal life grown by God's spirit in you—the best quality of life you can imagine. Likewise, if you sow good and healthy seeds, you will one day reap much more of the same. Again, this takes time. Sowing seeds doesn't make a big difference today, but the cumulative effect over a long period leads to significant change.

The key is not to grow weary and let the fatigue of the daily right decisions, with non-instant results, wear you out. Hang in there because, at the proper time, you reap a bountiful harvest if you don't give up. How many people plant seeds in life, water them, wait for what feels like forever, and then walk away in frustration a little too soon and never experience the fruits of their labor? What is proper, or due, time? God only knows that, but you know the wait is worthwhile when the harvest comes. I have repeatedly seen this play out, and I want that for you, too. So keep playing the tape to the end and remember that your decision to give in to temptation or to delay gratification for the future dream doesn't just lead you to a destination; it also shapes the person you become.

Tools to Help Overcome Temptation:

1. Write out your dreams and aspirations and hang them in a visible place.
2. When tempted by a bad decision, play the tape to see where it might lead.
3. Consider what you might be giving up to give in.
4. Ask God to give you strength to overcome.
5. Sow seeds through good choices for the future you wish to enjoy.

Chapter 24—Don't Lose at the What If? Game

As I look out my window right now and watch the sun poke through the faintest bit as the palm branches gently sway to a mild breeze, it's hard to believe that within a few hours, the sky will darken. Hurricane winds and rains from the dirty side of the storm will thrash upon our home. What if we lose power and internet coverage? What if the floodwaters make it into our home, and everything is ruined? What if the predicted tornadoes form and rip apart our home with our family inside? Even as I write these sentences, the sky has gone bleak, and raindrops trickle down, reminding us that the storm is coming for us. And I hate to tell you, but no matter where you live or your current conditions, a storm is coming for you, too. I don't know when, I don't know how big, and I don't know how much damage it will do. I only know you should expect a storm. As you read this, you may have started playing the "What If" Game."

Growing up, I loved the Marvel comic series *What If?* In it, a strange, bald, cosmic character called the Watcher considers what happens if a different choice or event occurs in the Marvel canon. For example, the premier issue explored "What if Spider-Man joined the Fantastic Four." The comic then told a butterfly effect story in which seemingly inconsequential changes morphed into wildly different and often catastrophic outcomes. Please forgive my indulgence in peak geekdom; I'll get to the point now. What makes for good entertainment can make your life miserable if you decide to play what I call the What If? Game poorly. Rather than reframing the past, many consider what if _____ (fill in the blank with whatever catastrophic thing you can think of) disrupts my future? It's a game you play all the time.

There is value in playing the What If? Game. Doing so enables you to look beyond the calm of your current circumstances to consider what threats might lurk that you can actually do something about. Yesterday, Rebecca and I moved our outdoor furniture inside, made sure we had enough supplies, and prepared for some of the potential threats the hurricane might bring.

In the same way, considering "What if?" can lead to wise preparations for the regular rhythms of life:

- "What if my job or financial situation suddenly changes?" can motivate you to start a rainy-day fund.

- "What if my health deteriorates prematurely?" can challenge you to start a fitness plan in which you eat healthier and exercise regularly.

- "What if my children get in with the wrong crowd and break bad?" can inspire you to train them about the power of relationships and how to discern the friends they should be and have.

- "What if something happens to my health or my home?" can nudge you to ensure you have the proper insurance coverage to provide for you and your family in the event of an unexpected loss.

Some bury their head in the sand and think, *It'll all work out somehow*. However, you can trust God to provide and plan wisely simultaneously. In this regard, playing the What If? Game can be of value to you, but you must consider it can also rob your enjoyment and peace if you go about it the wrong way.

The What If? Game turns nefarious when it moves you beyond consideration and preparation to fixation. Unlike the helpful path of looking ahead to challenges and planning for contingencies as best as possible, the darker version will have you fixating on the storm and its dangers. You play out the worst-case scenarios of every fear you have. So instead of the outcomes we discussed in the previous examples, you're begging for food on street corners, you're 800 pounds moving around on a scooter, your children are all in street gangs, and you died and your family was placed in debtor's prison. This happened in a day, and you freak out about it!

Fortunately, that scenario didn't happen, except in your mind. The bad news is that you are stressed out, your blood pressure is higher, and you are anxious and afraid because you are so worried that these things could happen. You asked, "What if?" and came up with real doozies that you are now terrified will become "what is."

Jesus asks you in Luke 12, *"What can worrying add to your life?"* and answers it can't even add a single hour to you. Not only does it not add anything, but anxiety subtracts things from your life, like joy, peace, contentment, sleep, and focus. It even bleeds from the mental and emotional and impacts your physical health. So why do you play the What If? Game in a way that leads you to lose at the worry game so severely? More importantly, how do you stop doing this?

I regularly refer to two verses to provide the exercise to deal with this. I encourage you to read them, memorize them, and then practice their explicit instruction: *"Do not be anxious about anything, but in every situation, by prayer and petition, with thanksgiving, present your requests to God. And the peace of God, which transcends all understanding, will guard your hearts and your minds in Christ Jesus"* (Phil. 4:6–7, NIV).

Let's break it down. *"Do not be anxious about anything."* Notice the "anything." Jesus told us worry adds no value to your life, so you need not practice it. By nature, some are more anxious than others. If that's you, you must lean into Jesus' instruction more intently. What lies underneath anxiety is fear—fear of bad things happening in the storms of life to you or the people you love, even when no storms are forecasted. Courage is not the absence of fear but moving forward in the face of fear. So, the goal is not fear elimination but refusing to let fear paralyze you. And the best chance you have to move forward courageously in the face of fear is by embracing faith.

This passage gives you a practical tool that unlocks a spiritual power to help you do this. *"But in every situation, by prayer and petition, with thanksgiving, present your requests to God."* The great news is this instruction applies to every situation or circumstance you are worried about; there are no exclusions. Instead of the useless and destructive practice of worrying, you are instructed to pray about whatever you are concerned about. I like to see this as turning your worry list into your prayer list. You are instructed on this—pray with thanksgiving.

It might seem strange to be thankful when you are terrified. Still, gratitude can cut away at fear. As you express appreciation to God for His good character and remind yourself of how He supernaturally intervened for you in the past, it fuels your trust tanks for what He can do in your life now as you *"present your requests to God."* You take your big concerns out of your limited hands and place them into the sufficient hands of the God who loves you deeply and has the power to handle anything. This is your part—replacing worrying with praying and transferring the burden to God. God's part in this is fantastic, and it is where the real impact happens. *"And the peace of God, which transcends all understanding, will guard your hearts and your minds in Christ Jesus."*

In anxiety, God offers you what you can't get for yourself—peace. This peace is bigger than your unresolved fears and guards your hearts and minds in Christ Jesus. Did you see that? God guards your heart (your emotions) and your mind (your thoughts). He restores to you all things that anxiety steals from you, which happens in the name and power of Jesus. It might help you to pause and pray right now.

Update #1:

It is now 24 hours after the hurricane made its way up the Gulf Coast, and a strange calm is on display from the view of my window. It's sunny, and the trees are still. We didn't lose power for even a second this time. The only telltale sign that anything happened is the small branch debris scattered across our lawn. It will take an hour to clean it up, and then you'd never be able to tell that a Category 4 hurricane passed through our city from my vantage point. Others we know were not so fortunate.

Update #2

It is five days after a major hurricane hit us directly, about two weeks after the previous storm. There were moments of fear and uncertainty, fought with prayer and preparation again. We lost power for a few days and still wait for our internet connection to be restored. Despite much more cleanup this time, our home had minimal damage, and my family is OK. Once again, many others were not as fortunate.

Worrying would have helped none of us. Playing the What If? Game properly helped us prepare for storm conditions and pray over the many things beyond our control. We are grateful for a sense of serene peace in the aftermath. We survived another storm, but we know more are on the unseen horizon. The same is true in your life. Don't worry; you know what to do.

Steps to Win the What If? Game:

1. Memorize Philippians 4:6–7.
2. Pray over whatever causes anxiety in you.
3. Release your worries into God's hands.
4. Receive the peace of God in your thoughts and emotions.
5. Thank God for what He has done and will do.

Chapter 25—Failing Forward

I stood in the stairwell between floors of the performance theater we rented for the launch of our new church location. This vantage point offered a view through the entrance windows to the cross streets where we hoped for 150 guests to come. People had given generously, prayed faithfully, traveled from West Hartford to Sarasota to be a part of the launch team, handed out invitations all over town, set up equipment and signs to transform a theater into a church, and trusted that God would bring many people to hear His word and be a part of an exciting new church downtown.

I stood in that stairwell 15 minutes before the service began and thought, *They'll be coming any minute.* I said the same thing 10 minutes before and then five minutes before. In sickened disappointment, I admitted to myself about five after, *They're not coming.* I then pulled myself together and preached my heart out to the small group gathered, which mainly included people we knew, coming to show their support. There were a few reasons we didn't gain traction. Still, I suspect it was primarily due to me, the lead pastor, flying back and forth from Florida to Connecticut to help two church locations thrive, but discovering my limits and realizing that despite immense faith and hard work, I was simply stretched too thin.

Several months later, to the disappointment of everyone involved, we concluded it was necessary to shut down the new location we attempted to launch and focus all our time and energy back on rebuilding the original location, which COVID-19 and the corresponding lockdown measures ravaged. I successfully launched a new church before, but I failed spectacularly this time, even with much more help and resources than the first time.

Failure is a one-two punch that not only knocks you out in the moment but can also discourage you from getting back up and into the ring. You still sting from the pain of defeat—the feeling that you let down everyone who believed in you—and because you justified your critics. You might sit in this place of failure because you stepped out and tried to do something big, but it didn't work. Or you knew this was the time you would overcome that bad habit, yet it overcame you once again. You can lie there busted up in disappointment and defeat or fail forward. I don't know who coined the phrase fail forward, but John Maxwell wrote a decent book on the topic. Regardless, the idea is self-evident; failing forward encapsulates the concept of failing but landing in a posture that positions you for advancement rather than one that pushes you backward or even leaves you standing still. By God's grace, I accomplished, achieved, and experienced successes I never thought possible. Yet, the reality is that the road to that was riddled with many failures, as it is for most. You must get up after the TKO and move again to fail forward. You may have your own strategy for this, but if you don't or your plan isn't complete, let me offer you a few ideas to help you pick up and keep moving. Remembering that failure isn't final, I present you with my TEMP plan to help you navigate past temporary failure and on to the wins in life that God has for you.

T in TEMP stands for transformation. Yes, you might not have achieved whatever goal or outcome you aimed for, but it helps to consider, "Did this effort or experience change me in some way?" For example, maybe you trained for a marathon that you could not finish or finished with a much longer run time than you hoped. Though you didn't meet your goal, did you accomplish other things? Were you more consistent with your training than in the past? Did you increase in speed? Did you learn to practice better rest and recovery cycles? Maybe you're white-knuckling your white chip, despairing that you relapsed after a long period of being clean. I've been there, and I know the pain. However, one moment of failure doesn't take away the days, weeks, months, or even years of clean time you had. It was real, and it is to be celebrated.

And I bet there were lessons you learned and tools you grabbed hold of this past season that can help you move forward into victory in this area of your life. Though you didn't get to where you wanted to be, how did you grow to get to where you are? While you came short of your goal, is there still transformation you experienced that can be celebrated? None of this is to justify your faults or shortcomings but to help you avoid destructive fatalism and see that even in failure, you can be refined, inspiring you to keep moving forward. This requires careful consideration of your failures.

E in TEMP stands for evaluation. It is the lynchpin of the entire plan. You've heard the expression, *"Experience is the best teacher."* I prefer the modified version, *"Evaluated experience is the best teacher."* When we held our weekly staff meetings at our church, we evaluated the Sunday service for improvement through four questions to celebrate the wins and improve regularly. If you want to understand a big, painful failure or want a diagnostic tool to evaluate your life events, I highly recommend you draw a quadrant of boxes. Next, write these four words, one in each quadrant:

Right
Wrong
Missing
Confusing

In each quadrant, answer these questions as you evaluate your specific failure.

In your attempt to _____ (you fill in the blank):

- What went right? (Acknowledging, celebrating, and repeating these things is essential.)

- What went wrong? (Brutal honesty is your friend here to discover what must be avoided in your next attempt.)

- What was missing? (These omissions in your execution could have been significant to failure and are critical to identify.)

- What was confusing? (Clarity is necessary, so identify hazy data points or action steps that can be more clearly expressed or implemented for achievements you aspire to.)

This isn't an easy exercise, especially if you leverage the prerequisite self-honesty needed for effectiveness. However, the information this process yields is absolute gold when planning your next push forward. The next step can help you with that.

M in TEMP stands for motivation. You have seen and experienced the difference between motivated and unmotivated people. Unmotivated people go through the motions of life even when doing something big, like starting a new chapter or quitting a bad habit. Motivated people, by contrast, are fueled with passion, bursting with energy, and do what it takes to get to the next level. This includes the process of evaluation and the difficult steps, one at a time, required for action to turn into momentum and eventually success. The problem is, especially after experiencing a deflating defeat, you might feel highly unmotivated compared to where you once were. The good news is that introspection can fuel your motivation to get up after failure and try again.

Ask yourself two critical questions: First, what am I trying to do? Again, clarity is king, so get very specific about whatever dream, goal, or target you are trying to achieve. The second question is even more important: Why do you want to do this? Here, you search for your motive, the keyword, and the key ingredient of motivation. You might answer with things like providing for my family, helping people in a specific way, glorifying God, etc. You probably have more than one core motivation, and that's OK. Write all these down to fuel you forward to launch and keep going when running against the wind. I have wanted to write a book my entire life and even had vague ideas about the concept. But it wasn't until I clarified what I wanted to do precisely and why I wanted to do it that I began to write it. You are part of my motivation for writing, and I want you to know that I sincerely appreciate your taking the time to read this and being part of the journey—which connects us to the last important point.

P in TEMP stands for participation. A transformative dream is never achieved alone; other people's participation in small and significant ways contributes to success. When Rebecca and I started the church we planted, we arrived alone in

Connecticut with our youngest daughter. Yet, we never could have achieved the dream without the participation of many more people than I could ever mention, but as an example, consider John and Suzanne. They attended another church that announced it would close shortly before we launched our church. When I spoke at that church, at the pastor's invitation, John and Suzanne were there and decided to come with us. They were a boost of encouragement and a powerhouse of support from the beginning. They helped set up and break down, John joined our leadership team, and Suzanne helped with lights (her specialty) and stage production, and in many other ways, even after one of my daughters peed on John when she was two years old!

Our hearts broke a few years in when John was suddenly diagnosed with and then died from Stage IV lung cancer; he was one of the kindest souls I have had the privilege to know. And yet Suzanne, who was there from the beginning, still plugged away faithfully serving God behind the scenes. Many people might not have noticed she was there, but everyone would have felt the difference if she didn't do what she did. John's time on Earth was short, but he worked hard to help build a church that, to this day, long after he and I were there, still bears fruit and does great things. Here is my point: Allow room for others to participate in what you do, and recognize and appreciate them regularly for their part in whatever success you achieve. It is vital that you also take part in what others are inspired to do and help them along the way with whatever support you might offer. In this way, you build others up and participate in the good things that might come from their dreams becoming a reality.

Defeat is only a TEMP situation, so regroup, get up, and get going because you don't want to be the fool who lets your previous chapter dictate the next chapter of your life. Learning from your mistakes might be the breakthrough that fuels greater success than you can imagine. Don't take my word for it; Google the invention of the pacemaker.

Steps to Move Past TEMP Failure:

1. **Transformation:** Consider how you grew stronger or better through failure.
2. **Evaluation:** Analyze what contributed to your failure and adjust.
3. **Motivation:** Clearly define what you want to do and why you want to do it.
4. **Participation:** Invite and appreciate others in your story, and offer to involve yourself in theirs.

Chapter 26—Victim, Villain, or Victor

Many video games let you select the type of character you want to play. A more novice player often chooses characters based on simple aesthetic appeal, but more experienced players consider their abilities before selecting. Is this character a damage dealer, a tank (to absorb damage), or maybe a healer to regenerate health? Yes, there are other roles and sublevels in each, but I am trying to keep my nerdiest impulses in check, and anyway, you get the point.

Whichever character you select—not just how well you play—helps determine the outcome. Real life is far more important than leveling up in a game; however, you must similarly choose your character and role, and the decision significantly affects your life. A better term than "a character" for you to apply this to yourself is "identity." So much of how you experience life is connected to your perceived identities, a topic we discussed. However, you should consider three more identity roles grouped in contrast to one another because of their prevalence and significant potential impact on you. Will you live your life as a victim, a villain, or a victor?

By nature, I am usually an optimist who sees the positive and the potential. So, it sometimes takes me longer to push aside the rose-colored glasses and see how grim things might actually be. Despite temperament, after considering your life's journeys, you may recognize bad things that happened to you or good things that should have happened or that you expected to happen but never did. Focusing on these hurts and disappointments makes it easy to feel sorry for yourself. And then, when you craft your narrative in a certain way, it's easy to make others feel sorry for you, too.

Nothing is wrong, and something is healthy with confronting the abuse, misuse, trauma, neglect, and other pain you dealt with in life and even telling others about the difficult things you experienced. However, when you don't grow past this but instead continue to rehearse your sad story to yourself and anyone who listens repeatedly, you choose a victim mentality for yourself through your beliefs and behaviors. Playing the victim might make people feel sorry for you, but it will never get you to the point of healing and prosperous living.

To be clear, you might have been victimized, and you might belong to a group of people who were historically oppressed, but that does not mean that must be your default identity. You have agency in whom you choose to become and need not select a self-limiting role. Living as a victim might get you short-term sympathy benefits, but the price you pay is too steep, as people who live as perpetual victims rarely flourish.

Think of the person you admire the most. Do you know their story? I bet that despite whatever success they might have experienced, the road to their achievement was hard and filled with many obstacles, challenges, failures and resistance to overcome. They didn't trade their potential for pity, and neither should you. There is a better way and a way that is just as bad. The person who lives as a victim constantly points out the villains in their lives who hold them back, but sometimes, you are the villain who holds yourself back.

You need not be Darth Vader, Ursula, or the Green Goblin to be a villain. After an honest inspection of your life, you see that bad things weren't done to just you; you did bad things to others. These might be small or even more significant things, which, by God's grace, you worked through with the injured party. However, you may have done vile, villainous things in your life for which your conscience convicts you as guilty and then wraps you in layers of shame. (Read chapter 35 which deals with toxic shame if that is you).

And just as it is important not to minimize how others victimized you, you must not minimize how you might have victimized others and, if possible, make things right. The problem is when, after reconciling or attempting to, especially when reconciliation is impossible, you continue to carry your sins and define yourself by them. Yes, you did those things. No, you should not excuse yourself from doing the things you did. But that doesn't mean you should don a dark cape and take on the villain identity.

When you see yourself as a villain, you'll find absolution for the past nearly impossible, and you'll also find it easier to keep doing things that add more weight to carry and reinforce your monstrous role. Villains do villainous things. But some of the best stories have a redemptive moment for the villain (hello, Anakin), and yours can be one of these. You can stop doing the things that caused you to identify or be defined as a villain and even shed the persona and baggage attached, but you need a new storyline.

Truthfully, I can go through my life story and craft a convincing narrative of myself as a victim just as quickly as I can assemble enough evidence for a convincing narrative starring me as a villain. Still, by entering God's story, a redemptive narrative has been crafted for me instead, and I emerge as a victor. Despite all my flaws and failures this is the narrative I embrace.

The victor identity can define you too, even if, until now, you lived as a victim or a villain. In Romans 8, which I highly encourage you to read regularly to discover who you are or could be if not yet a Christ follower, we are told this truth about ourselves: *"No, in all these things we are more than conquerors through him who loved us"* (Rom. 8:37, NIV).

In all what things? Well, considering the context of verses 31–39, "all these things" includes the fact that in Christ, God is for you; Jesus gave His life for yours; you are chosen; no one can bring a charge against you; Jesus died for you making you justified, not condemned; Jesus intercedes to God on your behalf;

160

and you cannot be separated from God's love. This is not just an amazing list of things that are true about Jesus' followers; these are also parts of a true identity rooted in Christ and include the fact that you are more than a conqueror or victor. This is who God designed you to be!

If you have trouble applying these truths to your life because of your current victim or villain identity framework, consider the author of Romans, the Apostle Paul. As Paul traveled the world to tell people about Jesus, he was severely victimized. Paul was ridiculed, beaten, stoned (rocks, not plants), imprisoned, had his rights violated, and was ultimately martyred for proclaiming God's good news. Yet, Paul also lived as an absolute villain for a season as he hunted down Christians and was complicit in the imprisonment and even the executions of many Christians before becoming a believer himself. He even described himself as the "chief of sinners."

Paul could have easily identified as a victim, considering that he wrote Romans and other New Testament writings from a prison cell. However, he refused to assume this identity and even wrote about experiencing joy and contentment in such circumstances. Likewise, Paul also could have easily slid into the villain role since he opposed God and victimized God's people, but living in that identity would have sidelined the man who wrote nearly half of the New Testament and greatly contributed to the birth of many churches and the spread of the gospel throughout the world then and now. Like Paul, you and I have a choice.

If you identified as a victim, remember the great sacrifice Jesus made to rescue you and for you to enjoy a life marked by victory. Remember that Jesus' death on the Cross atoned for your sins and for people who victimized you. This means ultimately, the ones who hurt you either find their redemption in Jesus, who paid for what they did on their behalf, or they pay the price themselves apart from Jesus for all eternity. Remember that you are deeply loved. You are not a victim anymore; you are a victor!

For my villains, remember that Paul was a God antagonist, too. Yet, God used him mightily for His purposes anyway. When your faith is in Christ, Jesus' death on the Cross means you are justified and no longer condemned. Never forget that you are deeply loved, too. You are not a villain anymore; you are a victor! Now, choose your character wisely and level up in life with a far more expansive and redemptive storyline than you could have imagined.

Steps to Living a Victorious Life:
1. Consider if, how and why you took on a victim identity role throughout your life.
2. Consider if, how and why you took on a villain identity role throughout your life.

3. Identify what steps you need to discard the victim and the villain roles you assumed.

4. Read Romans 8 and write down what God says about the victor identity role He wants you to live from.

Chapter 27—Maintain Integrity

Getting into our new home was a longer, wilder journey than expected. We sold our lovely but outgrown starter home. We signed a contract on a new home we thought would be wonderful until we discovered an undisclosed, buried pool in the backyard that one could still access via a door into a serial killer's paradise on the back end of a large hill. We backed out of that deal but were under contract to sell our current home, so we rented a townhouse while our search continued.

Six months turned into 18 months, but we finally found the perfect home in a great neighborhood with plenty of room for our growing family and room to extend hospitality to many guests. Aside from Rebecca slipping down the back deck stairs and being bedridden for a week, everything went smoothly until closing day. We arrived for our final inspection right before the closing, which we assumed would be a cursory walkthrough. We left in shocked disbelief as we headed over to what we knew would be a contentious meeting with the sellers.

One thing we loved about this house was the beautiful red oak floors that extended through the entire home. However, after a final inspection, we discovered everything was not as it seemed. Once the area rugs were removed in the living room, dining room, den, and bedrooms—you get it, all the rooms—we discovered that in each room, the flow was disrupted by a large pattern of a different type and color of wood in the center. It looked ridiculous and our hearts sank at the sight. To our shock, the seller was so offended when we asked him to fix the issue that he asked if I was on drugs. *"Not for many years,"* I deadpanned. Everybody was angry and upset, and we walked away from the table with incredible frustration in our hearts instead of the keys to our home in our hands.

As a home is a place in which you build your life; your being is where your soul exists, and you invite others into it. So, the questions you must consider are how you want to live and what you want others to experience when they enter your world. Rebecca and I were deeply disappointed that the home we wanted lacked integrity. The floors weren't a continuous flow of red oak hardwood, as we were led to believe, but instead, they had unattractive, disruptive patches all over the house.

The home also lacked integrity through deceit. The area rugs were carefully positioned to cover all the flaws and shabby patchwork to present itself as something it was not. Maybe if we had known about the Frankenstein floors, we could have lived with them or at least determined that we could fix them, but the cover-up was the most upsetting part.

People often feel the same way about others when they discover that they lack integrity in an area of their lives that looked in order, but upon closer inspection they find out this faulty area was covered up for appearances. You don't want others to experience the same disappointment because of an area in which you lack integrity. However, you shouldn't address it simply out of fear of what others might think if you were exposed. You and I ultimately are stuck living with ourselves, and we are far happier and healthier living a life marked by integrity than existing in one merely pretending to be. Living a life marked by integrity doesn't require perfection, but it does require intention. The first thing a life of integrity demands is regular examination. You don't wait until someone else removes your carpets and discovers your hidden flaws; instead, you can flip them over yourself to examine whatever you have hidden.

When the seller argued with us at the closing table, he said we should have known that the floors were in that condition before we signed the agreement. Our attorney effectively asked in rebuttal if we should have removed every painting on the wall to see whether the walls were in good order, too, and pointed out that there was a blatant attempt to conceal something that, in good faith, should have been disclosed. In the same way, you and I are responsible for pulling up the rugs to see what's hidden in our lives.

David prays a prayer of integrity that can also be helpful for us to adopt: *"Search me, God, and know my heart; test me and know my anxious thoughts. See if there is any offensive way in me, and lead me in the way everlasting"* (Ps. 139:23–24, NIV).

This is an examination prayer—a pulling-out-the-carpets prayer. When I speak of a lack of integrity, is there an area or issue that you struggle with that comes to mind? It might be in check now, but is it a temptation area? This is valuable information as you practice soul care. You are a complicated being, and there are likely unexamined areas in your life that you aren't even aware of which are problematic or offensive to God. That is why inviting God into the search process is so critical. He doesn't share your blind spots, self-preservation techniques, or limited insights; He sees everything. Remember that despite this, He still loves you deeply He loves you enough not to let you remain in this condition, so He presses in, uncovers, and exposes you in an uncomfortable but healing way.

I encourage you to put your hand in God's and let Him lead you on a journey to discover the deepest parts of yourself. It isn't always pleasant, but it is always redemptive if you trust God. A word of caution: Now that you have exposed yourself to yourself and God, telling everyone what you find is unnecessary and not even helpful. Not everyone can be trusted with your most sensitive self-discoveries, and not everyone needs to know. However, find someone you know and trust to share these things with. In 12-Step rooms, they say, *"You're as sick as your secrets,"* so why keep this to yourself?

James tells us *"Confess your sins to each other and pray for each other so that you may be healed..."* (James 5:16a, NLT). You need not tell everyone but tell someone what your examination uncovers. It would help if you also acted on this information.

After examination, you are ready for prayerful integration, where you do something about what you discover. In humility, invite God's help rather than doing it alone.

David offers another prayer, which you would do well to make your own: *"Teach me your way, Lord, that I may rely on your faithfulness; give me an undivided heart, that I may fear your name. I will praise you, Lord my God, with all my heart..."* (Ps. 86:11–12a, NIV).

Integrity refers to a state of wholeness. Thus, lacking integrity is a state in which division in your being interrupts your wholeness. So often, after we've examined our lives and uncovered our shortcomings, our first action can be to rush in to clean up whatever mess we've found. While you should want to deal with the issues rather than throwing the rug back on top, the mess will find its way back into your life if you only tidy up without dealing with the root cause.

That's why David asks God to give him an undivided heart, a whole heart, a heart of integrity. All the king's horses and all the king's men might not have been able to put Humpty Dumpty back together again, but God can put you together again, no matter how broken and divided you are. Ask Him! You need to participate in this process as you learn what it means to fear God in a healthy sense (basically, take Him seriously), rely on Him, and praise Him.

However, it is a fool's errand to do this without him. Reintegrating your soul might be difficult, painful, and messy work, like any construction zone. However, the result of living in wholeness and integrity with nothing to hide is worth the dirty journey to get there.

After a few days of backchannel communication, the seller finally agreed to pay for the floors to be fixed, and we closed on that home. The floors were redone before we moved in, but I stopped by a few times during the process. The crew worked hard, ripping everything out, then carefully putting in the new wood and finishing it until the result was the beautiful red oak hardwood floors throughout the home that we adored from the start. No patchwork!

Our family lived in that house for a decade and hosted many guests. We were all sad when we finally needed to say goodbye to this place filled with such precious memories. It was our favorite home we had lived in. You are the only place you will live in. I pray that through regular examination and prayerful integration, you and all guests into your world enjoy the beauty and peace a whole, undivided heart offers.

Steps to Rebuild Integrity:

1. Examination: Is an area of your life that you cover up in fear or shame of someone discovering.

2. Confession: Tell God and at least one other person you trust the truth about uncovered areas.

3. Integration: Ask God to repair this area of your life and reveal the steps required for you to live without "carpet cover-ups" in your life.

Chapter 28—Body Care Is Soul Care

Much time and effort were put into my sermon preparation as a pastor because I felt a responsibility to the people who sat on the other end of each message I delivered. If they would commit their time to come to our church hoping to hear a relevant, transformative word from God, wasn't I responsible for putting everything I could into sharing a biblically centered, God-inspired, creative, engaging message for them to receive? Crafting such messages typically took about 20–25 hours of prayer, thinking, study, writing, and rewriting. This time included reviewing my message notes for a couple of hours on Saturday night and a couple of hours early Sunday mornings to commit much of the message to memory before it was time to share publicly. After years of doing this, I experimented with something that permanently changed my Sunday morning routines. While recognizing the value of preparedness and diligence, I also felt that there were diminishing returns in reviewing notes repeatedly after a while and that it might be good to get in a different head space for a bit. So, one Sunday morning, I reviewed my notes for 30 minutes less than usual, laced up my running shoes, headed outside, and ran for half an hour. On the run, I prayed, asked God for wisdom, boldness, clarity, and so forth, and then just thought about things. Sometimes, as I continued this practice, I'd think of a new idea to incorporate into my sermon; other times, I simply enjoyed moving and getting my blood pumping. Another benefit was feeling terrific and having higher energy levels and mental clarity for at least a few hours after a run. This translated into a more engaging delivery of my messages. I would have never imagined that physical exercise could help me spiritually and intellectually, but it did, and it makes sense when we consider ourselves holistically.

We are not bodies who have souls, nor are we souls who have bodies. We are holistic beings God created to be body, soul, and spirit integrated together. And though, as followers of Jesus believe, our souls will eventually be separated from our present imperfect bodies and then dwell in perfect, eternal bodies, for now, our current bodies are important and interconnected to ourselves and God. Paul says this: *"Do you not know that your bodies are temples of the Holy Spirit, who is in you, whom you have received from God? You are not your own; you were bought at a price. Therefore, honor God with your bodies"* (1 Cor. 6:19–20, NIV).

There's a lot densely packed in there, but we will focus on your attitude about your body and your actions to respond to these great truths.

First, your bodies are the temples of God. That's a wild thought to consider! If you placed your faith in Christ, God's Holy Spirit resides inside you and goes with you wherever you go. You no longer have to go to a religious building to encounter

God; you are a religious building in which God lives. This should confront body issues and challenges you wrestle with. God is the author and creator of your body. Maybe you wish He had done some things differently. Maybe you wish you were shorter, taller, had a faster metabolism, a different pigmentation, straighter or curlier hair, more or less hair, different features, freedom from a disease or disability, or maybe even a different gender. As one who also struggled and questioned some of God's decisions for my body, I get it. But I am redirected when I consider that God has unique purposes for my life, which are included in His design for me, including my body. And rather than feeling shame, contempt, or disappointment for the body God gave me, I can learn to offer gratitude that God saw fit to give me life and a body and embrace appreciative amazement over the fact that He took up residence in this place I struggle to be in myself sometimes.

The price your life was bought with is the blood of Jesus. So since you are not your own, not only can you offer gratitude for your body, but you can also offer Him yieldedness. That looks like a conversation like this, *"God, you gave me a body; you live in my body, and in turn, I offer you gratitude and surrender to your design and all your purposes you wish to fulfill through the life you gifted me."* Coming to this mental and spiritual place with your physical body might take time. But if you commit to living this out and prayerfully ask God to help you, you can grow into living this way. As you learn to care about your body, you must also practice caring for your body.

One of my great regrets is not taking physical fitness more seriously in my younger years. This area is still a wrestle for me, so part of me feels like someone else should write this chapter. However, it's my book and important to discuss, so I'm giving it my best shot. As a young pastor, I used this verse as an excuse: *"For physical training is of some value, but godliness has value for all things, holding promise for both the present life and the life to come"* (1 Tim. 4:8, NIV). See, I reasoned, those gym rats needed to be in church more! Yet, while pursuing spiritual fitness has value in all things, there is still value in physical fitness.

As I discovered, it's all connected. The different parts of your being are not as compartmentalized as you sometimes like to believe. As Paul said, considering everything previously discussed about your body, *"Therefore, honor God with your bodies."* This moves you from body attitudes to body actions. How should you care for and maintain the house given to you by God, which He chooses to live in? How should you live so you can most effectively live out whatever God calls you to do in your lifetime?

I'm not a nutritionist or qualified to give medical advice, but at the very least, this charges you with the responsibility of being intentional with the inputs and outputs that impact your body's wellness. You are what you eat, we've all been told. That's a scary fact for Americans because we aren't sure what the heck is in our food supply, but we know that much of it is illegal in many other countries. For my family, this has led to our being more intentional in reading food labels before we buy groceries and tracking calories and macronutrients in fitness apps. We still eat junk food, but we limit it with the realization that food is the fuel we run on, so we want the best fuel to operate to the best of our abilities. What steps can you take to improve the food that enters your body? Are there immediate changes you can make for improvement? Along with nutrition is exercise; taking care of our temples requires both.

I didn't mention it earlier, but I kind of hate running. Yet, I still run at least twice a week because the benefits are great. My wife and I did Tae Kwon Do for a few years together, and despite injuring parts of us, it was an excellent exercise routine. And as the sign on the wall said, "The family that kicks together, sticks together." More recently we have traded our combat training for pickleball, but we still enjoy exercising together when possible. Weight training used to be something I hated, but now I go at least three times a week, even if you'd never notice it. I actually don't mind going to the gym now, and I love seeing and feeling the difference it makes in me. What can you do today to improve this area? Maybe even a few pushups, sit-ups, or jumping jacks? Maybe at least some stretching? Regardless, taking care of your body is integral to being the best version of yourself, so you have to figure out how to do it.

If you want to be healthy, tending to your body and not only your soul is essential. Body care is part of soul care because they are interconnected. This might already be an area of strength for you, so keep up the great work! If you struggle with how you view or treat your body, I want to encourage you to talk to God. He's not far from you. Ask Him to help you embrace the truths about your body that Scripture shares and learn to appreciate it. Then, eat and drink accordingly and get active in a way that makes sense for your current age, stage, and level of health and ability. Trigger those endorphins, release that stress, and prepare your body and health to be trained and ready for whatever God's next assignment for you might be.

Next Steps for Body Care:

1. Evaluate and write down how you feel about your body.
2. Thank God that He gave you life and a body, and confess to Him areas you feel shame over.
3. Write out a few actionable nutrition and exercise items you can implement right away to practice intentional body care.
4. Drop and give me 10! Push-ups, sit-ups, jumping jacks (or whatever you can do), anything that gets you moving.

Chapter 29—Always Practice Thankfulness

"Your smile confuses me," he said, genuinely intrigued. We were both lead pastors of local churches, both acquainted with the stresses and challenges regular church rhythms can bring, and he was aware of the extraordinary difficulties I navigated that season on top of everything else. Conflict, division, and difficult decisions abounded sufficiently, leaving me feeling dizzy, fatigued, and more than a little frustrated. Maybe I wasn't happy then, but I would let no one or anything steal my joy. There is a life lesson for us all in these three succinct New Testament verses I believe you'd be wise to commit to memory: *"Rejoice always, pray continually, give thanks in all circumstances; for this is God's will for you in Christ Jesus"* (1 Thess. 5:16–18, NIV).

People have always asked themselves, *"What is life all about?"* Or for the Christian, *"What is God's will for my life?"* Well, here you go; God wants you always to be full of joy, to be in prayer constantly, and to remain grateful despite your current circumstances.

Why would God want this for you and your life? To answer that, maybe it helps to consider the alternative: How does a lack of gratitude impact you? Instead of focusing on the things in your life for which you ought to be genuinely thankful, ingratitude leaves you to focus and even hyper-fixate on your circumstances, problems, challenges, inconveniences, pains, difficulties, and whatever stands between you and your happiness. The more these things become your focus, the less joy and gratitude you experience.

Maybe you pray anyway, but your prayers might turn selfish and angry. Prayer might be reduced to simply the list of things you want God to do for you, coupled with hints of frustration over your assessment that He doesn't seem to care or do anything about it. Or maybe you stop praying because you're angry with God or doubt His goodness or love for you because if you see all that's wrong in your life, surely He does, too. Yet He chooses to ignore it instead of changing it. When Jesus taught His followers to pray, He instructed them to ask God for their needs, but that is only a part that should be accompanied by praise, confession, submission, intercession for others, etc. God's desire for how you should live involves a better, healthier way for your soul to flourish as you learn to live in the flow of joy, prayer and gratitude.

You can maintain joy in your heart and a prayerful connection to God even when navigating through turbulent seasons of life. However, this is only your experience if you intentionally choose this path and take deliberate steps to walk on it. Here, gratitude as a discipline becomes essential. If discipline is too strong of a word for you, call it the practice of gratitude.

In my life, I find that practicing the three things in those verses in reverse order is key. Work on the thanksgiving piece, then take it to prayer, and the joy follows from there. Gratitude, not as an abstract concept but as a focused practice, might not change what you're going through, but it can radically change how you go through it.

Forgive the acronyms, but an APT way to live is to Always Practice Thanksgiving. In so doing, you can RISE above your circumstances and the unhealthy thoughts and emotions you might be susceptible to because of them and experience the joy your soul craves. RISE is the acronym for the discipline of gratitude I propose you enter. Yes, I am sorry that these acronyms are corny. At the same time, I'm confident you'll remember them now, so, you're welcome.

The R in RISE reminds you to Record everything you have to be thankful for. Yes, I highly encourage you to write these things down. When my daughters were younger and complained about things they were disappointed not to have, we sometimes asked them to write a gratitude list. I encourage you to do the same right now. Stop reading, take out a piece of paper, push aside everything you don't have or that doesn't seem to be going your way, and record everything you are blessed with. Write down at least 20 things. I bet you can do 50 without trying too hard once you get going. If you're in a dark place, maybe write down things you've been historically grateful for and then move closer to the present to record what you appreciate now.

The I in Rise reminds you to Internalize everything you wrote down on your list for which you are thankful. The first step is to take the list you created and display it where you will regularly see it, like a bathroom mirror, desk, nightstand, or wherever else you can think of. Your difficulties always strongarm your mind for attention, so you must intentionally offer your brain something else to ruminate on.

So now, with that practical list accomplished, take the time to do precisely that: Meditate on everything you have to be grateful for so you can internalize these things into your soul. You retrain your brain as you reorient your focus and set the stage for transformative feelings. For example, take your body. We already discussed how you might have issues with your body. But instead of complaining about what you consider defects, celebrate the right things.

Does your body at least function and enable you to move, work, play, accomplish, and experience things in life? Maybe you have disabilities or diseases that make these things more challenging for you than most. Is there some way your body works well and lets you sense and enjoy special things? Or how about your being born and having a body, considering your birth and life is a statistical miracle of that sperm meeting that egg at the right time?

Now, work down your gratitude list and have these conversations in your mind. Sometimes, they might challenge and put your mental complaint list in check, which is terrific. But even if they don't, you're still left with new thoughts to ponder and celebrate. As your gratitude emerges, it must be passed along to grow.

The S in RISE reminds you to Share your gratitude with others after recording and internalizing what you are thankful for. You can do this in several ways, and perhaps you'll think of more examples than the ones I offer. People often ask, *"How are you?"* and if you are close enough to them not to respond with the obligatory "fine," you might tell them all your current struggles and frustrations.

It is healthy to unburden yourself and invite others into your world, so I don't suggest you stop doing that. But what if you also included and maybe even started with two or three things you're thankful for? Sharing gratitude shouldn't be reserved for passive responses, but you can be intentional about these things. How about leveraging your social media presence to share things you're thankful for today? How might that brighten someone's day whose timeline is otherwise filled with bad news about everything wrong with the world and complaints about the culprits responsible for it?

A sharing practice I've been more intentional about lately is an instant appreciation contact. If I remember that I am thankful to someone for something, I'll instantly call or text to let them know how much I appreciate them, especially if I have until then failed to do so.

The E in RISE reminds us to Express gratitude to God. We mustn't forget God in all this, so I make it a practice to begin my prayers with praise and thanksgiving to God before I get to my requests, as a measure to fight back my selfish impulses and give God the glory He deserves. This can be as easy as taking out that gratitude list daily and thanking God in prayer for a few items on it. Let Him know that despite everything else going on in your life, you recognize His goodness and appreciate His gracious hand at work in your life, even during the bumpy parts of the ride.

Sharing thanksgiving with others warms the hearts of those on the other side of your gratitude and reinforces thankfulness in your soul. And yes, the joy it brings might leak out of your heart, even as the world burns, in the form of a confusing smile on your face.

Steps to Always Be Thankful:

1. **Record**—Write a gratitude list.
2. **Internalize**—Meditate on the things for which you are thankful.
3. **Share**—Tell others what you are grateful for, including them.
4. **Express**—Thank God in your prayers for all the goodness in your life.

Chapter 30—Good Grief

My friends still laugh at my expense about the cat poop incident. To be fair, I am much more a dog than a cat person, though I concede that kittens are cute. My roommate Jason had a cat named Peapod, who eventually became insane. One night, Jason was out, and I was busy writing a final essay due the following day for one of my courses. Having procrastinated until the last moment, I raced against the clock.

As I jammed away on the keyboard, I noticed the crazy cat had relieved himself on the living room carpet. Peapod's inconsiderate act placed me in quite a predicament because I was under timebound pressure and in the zone with my writing, and yet I knew that doing nothing about it would be irresponsible. So I got the Lysol, sprayed the turd to mask the foul odor, covered the mess with a paper towel so nobody would see the unsightly pile, and got back to business. When my roommate came home hours later, he disturbed me from my writing to ask, *"Why didn't you just pick it up?"* *"Bro, I was busy"* seemed like a justifiable response. It took years for me to realize that this was also my approach to handling grief.

Why do the hard, smelly work of processing through grief when you can instead cover up the sight, smell, and every other unpleasant reminder of the people or things you lost? Sure, sometimes, something reminds you, and you shed a tear or endure a visceral emotion, but to sit down and actively process your grief? Who has time for that?

"Bro, I was busy," we might all say in our own ways to dismiss our lack of intention in this area. Grief is never convenient and always interrupts your life, seemingly at the worst of times. Yet a compelling reason to make the time to deal with it is for your mental, emotional, and spiritual health.

When you cover up your grief, it doesn't simply go away; it digs down into your heart and mind and manifests itself in thoughts, behaviors, actions, and attitudes you might not readily associate with grief. Depression, anger, desperation, hopelessness, anxiety, codependency, and more can be things you have to deal with because you avoid direct confrontation with grief. And because these, too, are difficult to handle, many choose to cover up these symptoms with eating, shopping, entertainment, working, porn, drugs, alcohol or whatever distracts you from what you're too "busy" to deal with.

I know this contributed to my brokenness. Did unprocessed grief lead me to drug abuse? No. But was it a contributing factor? I'm sure of it. Likewise, your unprocessed grief may help to cause greater damage to your soul than you realize. The problem is, like anything you shove into your soul to avoid dealing with, grief not only doesn't go away, but it also distorts itself and becomes more toxic.

Maybe that's part of your problem; you're afraid of what you will find when you rip off the paper towels and see what horrors await. If you want to be well, you must also be brave.

Most of us are familiar with the five stages of grief: denial, anger, bargaining, depression, and acceptance. You are probably aware that these "stages" rarely occur in a neat, linear way but are messy, cyclical, overlapping, and can happen over a sustained period. These are difficult things to go through, which is why many of us try to get around rather than walk through these things directly. It is challenging because we can't just check each stage off the box and move on to the next on our timelines as if grief were a module to work through. Grief takes as long as it takes and exists in a form and fashion we can't organize for convenience. Yet, as hard as it is, Solomon (the wisest man who lived in his time) had this to say about grief: *"It is better to go to a house of mourning than to go to a house of feasting, for death is the destiny of everyone; the living should take this to heart"* (Eccl. 7:2, NIV).

Cheery, right? Yet, it helps remind you that going through the process of grief adds much more value than partying and carrying on as if everything is fine when it isn't. I don't mean to let go of true joy, as you can maintain joy even in hard times, but I do mean intentionally pressing into the uncomfortable. If you need a refresher on navigating the stages of grief, I encourage you to do a simple Google search and learn what you need to walk through. I offer you an exercise that helps you clarify why you need to do it.

When Rebecca and I left the church we spent nearly two decades pouring ourselves into, we had sabbatical guides prepared to process the past, navigate our new present, and explore the future. Wisely, Jen, the spiritual director who prepared our guides, packed in a fair bit of content and exercises to help us walk through our grief. One practice I greatly benefited from, which will be of great value to you, was called Naming Your Goodbyes.

When someone we love dies or a close relationship is severed, it is reasonably clear to us that a grieving process and period are required. Yet, you and I have experienced and will experience many losses over our lifetimes. These losses range from tiny to catastrophic, and yet, despite the size, the cumulative effect of these losses unprocessed can be disastrous for us. This is why it is important to name your goodbyes, whether the goodbye is to a person, a season, a stage of life, a dream, a hope, or whatever it might be.

During this exercise, I wrote down many things our family was saying goodbye to—silly, significant, all of it. We said goodbye to the church we started, the people we loved, a town/community we loved, the house our girls grew up in, our staff team, ministry objectives, a job, a purpose, a mission, our Tae Kwon Do school, the best pizza, cool fresh air and drinking water, processing and burning firewood, youth, a plan for career to retirement, etc. Many more items were on my list, but you get the point. Admittedly, some things on my list, and most likely yours, might seem relatively insignificant compared to the weightier goodbyes, but you miss them, and it is healthy to recognize that you do.

While I'm on the topic, comparison can be a grief obstacle if you aren't careful. Not only might you compare the smaller goodbyes in your life to the bigger ones and consider them insignificant, but you might compare your entire stack of goodbyes to someone who had much more significant loss than you have and, in a false nobility, dismiss your goodbyes as less important. Don't compare; write down all your losses or goodbyes, and then carefully, prayerfully lean into the stages of grief. Some goodbyes are quick and not too horrible; others take serious time and sometimes feel excruciating. Keep at it; healing is on the other side of the pain and hard work.

As grief comes in waves, so does joy. I encourage you to go through your goodbye list and glean a deeper understanding of God, yourself, and your circumstances as you do. I observed that everything I grieved in that season was first a blessing from God which flowed from the mission He directed us into. Even with tears of grief, I thanked God for letting us have and experience what we were saying goodbye to.

In the words of the prophet Dr. Seuss (supposedly), *"Don't cry because it's over; smile because it happened."* I caveat this by

187

saying the not crying part is counterproductive, terrible advice, as grief is a healing medicine for the soul. However, the smile because it happened part is sage advice, especially as it allows for gratitude and joy amid anguish.

It's kind of like a funeral service. The best memorials always give space for guests to share eulogies (stories or memories) to celebrate the departed's life. In these stories, tears are always mixed with laughter, reminding you how sad you are to have lost someone you loved so dearly but how thankful you are that they were part of your life.

Similarly, after a season of processing, Rebecca and I held a funeral service for the past season we let go of, also at the recommendation of Jen, and it was painful but healing. It might help you to do this exercise, too, at the time that seems right to you, as you move from naming your goodbyes to saying your goodbyes to whatever or whomever you lost.

Don't tell Jason, but years later, I'm coming around to his perspective. May today be your day to slow down from busyness, put away the Lysol and paper towels of cover-up, and lean into the messy, therapeutic grief process.

Steps to Process Grief:
1. Name your goodbyes; write down a list of lost things you have never grieved.

2. Resist the urge to dismiss your losses by comparing with others.

3. Accept discomfort as you prayerfully and bravely mourn over your losses.

4. Notice your feelings and ask God to help you navigate through them.

Chapter 31—Mystics and Discipline

I considered the invitation with a skeptical curiosity. As a pastor, I received many invitations to attend various conferences on leadership, strategic systems, best practices, and so forth, but this unique opportunity called pastors to come and experience "Spiritual Formation" differently. This sounded good and wise, as pastors leading churches should grow deeper in faith and are usually on the giving side of spiritual development, but I was hesitant. One thing people who aren't Christians find confusing and sometimes frustrating is that we come in many varieties of theology and leanings. I sympathize with the curious tire-kicker or even the newer Christian trying to learn the ropes, but I generally find this good. It means that under one tent, many tribes are trying to figure things out together.

Despite the infighting among these tribes and the insistence among some that only their tribe has the corner on truth, I appreciate that there is always a place someone finds to belong. We can learn something from each tribe, even though we disagree on some issues. The retreat invitation I considered was from a tribe called The Mystics. (They probably don't call themselves that, but I did.) Those strange folks followed ancient sacred practices that fell outside the standard staples many are familiar with like praying, reading the Bible, and attending church.

Yet I deeply respected Vision New England, who recommended and sponsored this. So, their credibility and the free-to-me cost pushed me to accept the invitation. I am so glad I did.

After arriving at the Rolling Ridge Retreat and Conference Center in North Andover, MA, I marveled at the impressive courtyard that led into an even more remarkable mansion. I met my "fellow travelers" (the Mystics say cool things like that) and eventually met the mystical gurus (they certainly wouldn't call themselves that), Doug and Adele. We all shared a nice meal, and then it began. Instead of spontaneous prayers, prewritten, intentionally selected prayers were offered before and after each session. Candles were lit and blown out to signal clear beginnings, ends, and transitions. There was a lot of talk about pressing inside ourselves. There was even a day when we were not to speak to anyone as we practiced the discipline of silence; if you know me, you know how challenging that was.

As time passed, I lowered my guard. To my surprise and delight, I felt God doing deep work within my soul as I was guided into new practices that were strange to me but not necessarily strange altogether. Through several of these gatherings, I learned the concept of the Enneagram and what that revealed about God and me. The importance of doing some of the inner healing work was impressed upon us. I became aware of my need to press into places I glossed over with a Bible verse and a prayer but never let God heal.

A great benefit is that not only did I have a transformative experience at each gathering, but I also left with new practices to go deeper in soul and Spirit each day on my own. While I might not be a spiritual guru, I share three of my favorite spiritual disciplines (or soul practices, if you prefer) to get you started and a recommended resource to help you go further on this journey.

1.   The Examen

The Examen is one of my favorites of the spiritual disciplines I learned. Also known as The Examination of Consciousness, the Examen helps you notice where and how God shows up in your day. It's a practice for discerning God's voice and activity within the day's flow. The goal is to help you "keep company" with Jesus throughout the day.

If you're like me, you might pray at the beginning and end of the day and yet often fail to notice God or even your soul throughout the day and miss the connection of the two. The Examen is a practice designed to develop more discernment and receptivity to God's voice daily. It is also a tool to foster gratitude, a topic so important that it has its own chapter in this book.

It involves your setting aside time each day to notice and reflect. What are the consolations and desolations in your soul each day? Said differently, what are the things that brought you joy today, and what brought pain or distress to your heart today?

Peter Scazzero, in his book *Emotionally Healthy Spirituality*, recommends five basic steps, one of which is "Review the day with openness and gratitude, looking for times when God has been present, and times you may have ignored Him." This is the key to the exercise, and I want to simplify this because you don't need to overcomplicate this practice for it to be effective.

When I walked my daughters through this practice, I asked them to answer two questions around the dinner table: *"Where did you see God at work today, and what are you grateful for?"* At first, they gave silly answers, but some real gems emerged. And here is the beauty of this practice. When you know that you will ask yourself or a group of "fellow travelers" these questions, you begin to notice more things throughout the day that you might offer that evening. Success!

The whole idea is that you start noticing. Even on the worst days, God might have shown up, and even if you have to look hard, there is probably something for which you can express gratitude to God. And if you have trouble answering these questions positively, that, too, reveals areas you can press deeper into in prayer. Socrates said, *"The unexamined life is not worth living."* The practice of the Examen helps you live with an intentional examination every day you practice it.

2. Lectio Divina

Another practice I have significantly benefitted from is Lectio Divina. These practices with Latin titles sound much more impressive, don't they? In English, it means Divine Reading, an old monastic practice for Scripture reading that is more prayerful and contemplative than many of us modern-day folks are accustomed to. According to most online sources, the basic moves of the Lectio Divina are Prepare (silencio), Read (lectio), Meditate (meditatio), Pray (oratio), and Contemplate (contemplatio).

You can read the selected passage of Scripture before each step or as the first and final steps. You do not read simply to study, nor is it quick passive reading. It is about taking the time to prayerfully understand what the Scriptures are saying and what you sense God is trying to tell you through this passage.

How I practice this, and how I recommend you begin if you feel you would benefit from this, is through an app called Lectio 365. I preferred to listen to it, but you can read the daily prayers, pauses, and reflections if you prefer. This practice enriched my daily Bible reading and prayer, and the app often features people with European accents reading, which makes the readings sound more spiritual! If you prefer to go it alone, a basic search will yield many good online articles to guide you through this practice.

3. Silence

The last practice I want to mention here is Silence. As I said, this is challenging for me, but it is also highly beneficial. I am addicted to noise. I talk a lot, consume a lot of news and other media, and like loud music. Something constantly interrupts the quiet and fills that space with noise in my life. You live in the same world I do and probably carry the greatest distraction/noisemaker in the history of the world (the smartphone) with you wherever you go, like me. So, even if you're an introvert, I bet a lot of noise comes your way, even if you're rarely the one making it.

The practice of Silence is a simple yet strong pushback to modern madness. It helps you step back for a defined chunk of time so you can hear the quiet cries of your longing soul and the whisper of God you say you want to hear but constantly drown out with a steady stream of inputs and outputs.

Though Silence is one of the most straightforward practices to understand, it isn't easy to do because it is so foreign to our modern way of life. To set yourself up for success, select a length of time. Maybe start with an hour. If you're ready to level up, practice this for a day. If you go for a week, you're basically a monk or much more spiritual than I am, so congrats.

It is essential to let those closest to you know what you're doing. Otherwise, they might become concerned or annoyed when you don't speak to them. It isn't just about not speaking verbally, so confront that addiction and turn your phone on DND, or even better, turn it off. News, notifications, messages, and alerts are all part of the noise you need to turn off for the sake of your soul.

So what do you do? Silence is a practice best paired with other practices. So read, journal, pray, and practice the Examen or the Lectio Divina. Take a walk on the beach or park or light a candle, and contemplate in a cozy corner somewhere. You may be among the majority addicted to the dopamine hits your devices give you, but in Silence, you can get in touch with the deeper desires of the soul and with the God who supplies and satisfies your healthiest desires.

Accepting the invitation to the Spiritual Formation event and being part of that network for over a year was the right call. It equipped me with new information and practices to enrich my soul and connect me deeper with God. I hope you now accept my invitation to practice some of these spiritual disciplines you possibly never heard of or dismissed as too weird or mystical in the past.

A field guide I recommend you get to help you navigate through this is the *Spiritual Disciplines Handbook* by Adele Calhoun. It is a treasure trove of spiritual practices with explanations and recommendations on implementing these into your life. Adele and her husband, Doug, helped me understand myself and God better than I had, and I trust this practical, spiritual resource might do the same for you, too. So now I pass the invitation on to you.

Steps to Practice Spiritual Formation:

1. Consider your current spiritual formation practices and evaluate which are helping you grow and connect more deeply to God.
2. Practice the Examen for one month and determine if it would help you to continue longer.
3. Practice Lectio Divina for one month and determine if it would help you to continue longer.
4. Practice Silence for one hour, then work up to one day and consider how often this might help your soul.
5. Get a copy of *The Spiritual Disciplines Handbook* and experiment with different practices to help you in spiritual formation.

Chapter 32—Don't Make the Cheap Trades

We both looked at one another's toys with envy. I had a Tonka truck that my mother had given me as a birthday gift, but my friend sported a Tyrannosaurus Rex replica. After a fierce round of negotiations, we traded toys, shook hands, and then played with our newfound treasures. Later that afternoon, the boy's mother found me, and to her credit, she wanted to confirm that I had agreed to this deal. She explained the toy I gave her son was much more valuable than the cheap plastic figure he had given me in exchange. *"Are you sure you wanted to do this?"* she asked, giving me every opportunity to back out of the deal. *Woman, you're talking about a T-Rex!* I thought before confirming, *"Yes, ma'am."* And so I made the first of many foolish trades in my life.

Did you ever end up on the bad end of a deal? It is a horrible feeling to realize someone suckered you in and ripped you off. Even now, I can think of a few that would cause my blood pressure to go up if I allowed myself to think about them for too long. A more helpful exercise than seething over the shysters who got you along the way is to consider your foolishness in the bad, cheap, short-sighted trades you have made and learn from them so you don't keep repeating variations of the raw deals and continue to constantly rip yourself off.

To help you see this better in yourself, let's first look at a classic example of doing this. Jacob and Esau were contentious brothers, nipping at each other's heels from birth. Jacob was the homebody mama's boy, and Esau was the hunter macho man. One day, Esau returned famished from a hunt and smelled the lentil stew his brother was cooking. Esau emphatically demanded a bowl of stew, to which Jacob shrewdly made his own demand—Esau's birthright (shyster alert!). Esau gave a tragic comedy of a response: *"Look, I am about to die. What good is the birthright to me?"* (Gen. 25:32, NIV).

After Jacob received the proper assurances of a binding deal, the exchange took place: *"Then Jacob gave Esau some bread and some lentil stew. He ate and drank, and then got up and left. So Esau despised his birthright"* (Gen. 25:34, NIV).

In a moment, a meal was consumed, an appetite was temporarily satiated, and a glorious future was flippantly forfeited. And so it is with you with the cheap trades you make in life.

"What good is a birthright to me if I die of starvation?" Esau posits. What's easy to see in his "logic" is that he has elevated his appetite to the point of absurdity. Yes, Esau was probably hungry, but he wouldn't have keeled over dead in minutes if he didn't eat a bowl of beans immediately.

You must consider the immense value of a birthright at that time to understand his absurdity. The birthright was given to the firstborn son, and it entitled the holder to the lion's share of the family fortune and leadership as an inheritance. A birthright was tremendously valuable, but it had one challenge—you had to wait a long time before it offered you its full value. But a hot meal with a side of buttered bread to satisfy your hunger pangs was something you could have right then.

And so it is with you when you trade away long-term blessings for instant gratification and the satisfaction of baser appetites. We could examine many areas of life where you do this, but let's consider two areas most of us really like—food and sex. Then, we'll talk about how you can become a better trader in all things.

I have been a big fan of food for as long as I can remember, partially explaining my lifelong struggle with maintaining a healthy weight. As many have noted, the issue is unlike other bad habits because abstinence is not an option in this area. You have to eat to live. However, how and what you eat is an option for most of us, which is great. What isn't so wonderful is what many do with those choices.

Processed foods make up almost 70% of the food Americans consume. Why? It's a combination of convenience, cost, availability, taste, and habit that keeps us locked into a diet of poor nutrition even when we track other factors like calories and macronutrients. And this cheap trade comes at a serious cost. Americans suffer in record numbers from obesity, metabolic and cardiovascular diseases, cancer, and psychological effects, much of which comes from the fake food we eat. Junk food calls out to us from everywhere! I am no health nut, but I need not be to point out the trade-off. You enjoy a quick, delicious, but not very nutritious, snack or meal. In exchange, you trade looking and feeling your best and expose yourself to many unnecessary health risks and diseases. You trade your birthright for a bowl of stew. Or a bowl of triple peanut butter ice cream if you're me.

Sex is another area where cheap trades are often made. Unlike food, you need not engage in sexual activities to live, but you have powerful natural desires that might make you feel that way. And sex is required to keep the human population going and growing. So sex, like food, is a natural and necessary experience you must navigate your relationship with. But it is also one where many birthrights have been signed over collectively in poor choices and instantly in moments of out-of-control, intense appetites.

Part of this relates to the cheap plastic trade I mentioned in the beginning. Sex, by design, is an act of intimacy. But intimacy can be traded for cheap, phony gratification with a few clicks on a computer or even the phone you carry wherever you go. The porn industry is estimated to generate almost $100 billion yearly, which shows its massive worldwide demand. Yet the costs of pornography are also huge—guilt, shame, fear, and reduced capacity to experience intimacy.

Cheap trades are also made when people sacrifice their committed vows of faithfulness to their spouse. About 50% of marriages end in divorce, and of those, somewhere between 20% and 40% are severed because of infidelity. The dreams of growing old together, hand in hand, get shredded because one partner's momentary desire overshadows their long-term hopes and dreams. *"Look, I am about to die (of lust). What good is a birthright to me?"*

Both food and sex could be explored in much greater detail along with other areas in which we are often tempted to make cheap trades, but for our purposes here, let's focus on what you can do to protect your birthright by trading, or not trading, wisely. Always remember to weigh value and cost. Esau's desire for instant gratification pushed him to skip this important step, but you can learn from his mistake to take the time to do this.

Consider what the value is. What do you actually get from this trade, this bowl of stew? With that in mind, consider the cost. What might you be trading away even in the future to satisfy this appetite now? Now compare. Which do you value more? Still ready to grab the lentils?

I heard a sermon Charles Stanley gave about Esau decades ago, and I've never forgotten it. In it, he offers a tool that slows us down and reminds us not to make important decisions under certain circumstances but instead HALT! Don't make critical decisions when you are Hurt, Angry, Lonely, or Tired. Slow things down and let time be your friend. While you wait, perhaps take the time to seek wise counsel. Bad decisions are often made in the darkness and in a vacuum. Take the time to bring your decision to light by presenting it to someone who evidences a history of wisdom in the decision area you are contemplating. If Esau had taken the time to talk to his father, he would have reminded his son how valuable the gift awaiting him really was. In the same way, you can always talk to your Father in Heaven without any shame: *"If any of you lacks wisdom, you should ask God, who gives generously to all without finding fault, and it will be given to you"* (Jas. 1:5, NIV).

Finally, when instant gratification gives you tunnel vision, expand your perspective by zooming out. Imagine if Esau had stopped before he made the deal to picture himself leaving the house with a full stomach and an empty pocket where his birth certificate used to be. Would he have so readily regarded his future inheritance as equivalent to the meal that would soon be eliminated from his body as waste? Sorry to be somewhat graphic, but we need to get real and get raw to wrestle past improper satiation of our burning appetites.

If you are anything like me, you greatly regret some poor trades in life. Unfortunately, we don't get a redo on those trades. The good news is we can learn from those experiences, walk in greater wisdom, and refuse to make any more cheap trades going forward.

Steps to Evaluate Trades:

1. Weigh value and cost.

2. Instantly HALT.

3. Seek wise counsel.

4. Zoom out to expand your perspective.

Chapter 33—Freedom in Forgiveness

One exercise I went through at Calvary House was called Houses. On a whiteboard, we were to draw the homes we lived in growing up and then write key events, good and bad, that happened in each. Then, a group of our fellow recovering drug addicts would make observations about our lives. What could possibly go wrong?

As I presented my houses with non-pausing efficiency, one guy said, *"Wait, back up. You kind of casually mentioned the part about your stepfather beating your mother and then just moved on. Have you ever forgiven him?"* His question seemed absurd, which was reflected in my response. *"Absolutely not; he doesn't deserve it. He treated my precious mom like a bag of trash, and I hate him; let's move on,"* I said in the same matter-of-fact way you might share a daily weather forecast. To his great credit, he pushed back at me, saying, *"You have to forgive him. Jesus tells you that you must. And if you refuse to, you'll stay stuck emotionally and probably keep repeating the same behaviors that got you here in the first place."*

Another person who has walked the same path of brokenness as you can call you out with greater speed and precision than just about anyone else. Though he was dead right, I had a difficult time even contemplating releasing this unforgiveness that I packed and carried with me everywhere I went for my entire life. Yet this loving confrontation got my head buzzing, and I couldn't shake off the thought that though I didn't know how I could forgive, maybe it was time to let this burden go.

It's not a big leap for me to assume you have a story in your life of an offense that is simply too big to forgive. Maybe something awful was done to you or someone you love that is still painful for you to consider. If it's a fresher wound, you might feel the fresh sting of pain even now. If the wound is older, the hurt might have scarred into anger, and you might be seething even as you read this sentence

The offense you find difficult to forgive could be a sin of omission. Did someone who should have protected you, provided for you, cherished you, defended you, or advocated for you neglect or even abandon you? The pain of absence can be as powerful as the pain of offense. And since we're being real, maybe the culprit you struggle to forgive is the same face that greets you in every reflection. Perhaps you have done something so terrible or unspeakable or neglected to do something you should have done that the unforgiveness and the hate you feel inside are directed back at you.

I know I'm likely stirring up some uncomfortable things in you. I do not disagree that you have a right to hurt, anger, or whatever else you might feel. However, in the paraphrased words of the man who challenged me in my Houses, if you do not deal with this head-on, you will stay stuck, remain emotionally and spiritually immature, and repeat familiar, unhealthy, and self-destructive patterns of coping to the detriment of those around you and yourself.

It's difficult to forgive, but you should at least acknowledge that it might be even more difficult to choose to not do so. I'm not sure Nelson Mandela first said this, but someone did, and it is poignant: *"Unforgiveness is like drinking poison and waiting for the other person to die."* That's good. Jesus also had some freeing thoughts on this subject.

Peter asked Jesus how often one should forgive an offender. Perhaps Peter thought himself generous and worthy of a gold star when he suggested up to seven times. Imagine Peter's surprise when Jesus countered 77 times, essentially saying there is no real quantifiable limit on forgiveness. I can see perplexed Peter wrestling through this moral dilemma in the same way we try to understand how we could ever forgive what has been done to us. Jesus often taught heavenly truths in simple, digestible stories that the everyday person could understand, so he took this occasion to tell one story involving servants and a master.

I encourage you to read Matthew 18:21–35 to mine this gem of a parable for all its riches for yourself, but let me offer you a summary. A servant owes a master more money than he could repay in a lifetime. The master is about to condemn the man to prison for the debt, but the servant begs for mercy. Having pity, the master not only releases the man from custody but also from

207

his debt. Imagine how liberating it felt to have all the weight upon you removed!

However, this same servant then sought a man who owed him maybe a day's wages and demanded immediate repayment. The other servant then fell to his knees and begged for more time to settle the debt. In this moment, the recently liberated servant should have seen himself in this man and empathized, having recently been in the same position for a much lighter debt. However, the man had this other guy imprisoned for lack of repayment.

Just as you and I are outraged thinking about this, so were the other servants who saw this and reported to the master. The master was so angry with the servant who refused to extend the same mercy he recently received that he put the debt back on to this merciless servant and had him locked up until the debt was repaid. Then Jesus adds this commentary to His story: *"This is how my heavenly Father will treat each of you unless you forgive your brother or sister from your heart"* (Matt. 18:35, NIV).

A prison, a poison, whatever you want to call it, unforgiveness destroys freedom and slowly kills the one who refuses to let it go. Forgiving may be freeing and life-giving, but it is difficult in practice, even when we principally understand its importance.

A few days after being confronted with the need to forgive, I determined to forgive my stepfather, even though the thought of doing so still filled me with extreme displeasure. I had to take two important steps for this to happen, and I would like to share them with you in hopes that they help you in your journey of forgiveness.

The first thing I had to do was to choose to forgive. Yes, the underlying feelings that justified my unforgiveness were intense and maybe even justifiable. But feelings, while important, could not be left alone to make this decision for my life. I had to recognize that forgiving my former stepfather did not mean I had to excuse his behavior or even reactivate a relationship with him. It simply meant I needed to close the ledger of the debt he owed. The forgiven person benefits, but part of the reason to make this decision is your own well-being. You need to stop carrying this baggage to experience true freedom in life.

A phrase I coined to capture what Jesus shared in His story on forgiving is "freedom grows where forgiveness flows." If I want freedom, then I need to get into its flow. When I consider all Jesus forgave me of, like that wicked servant, then how could I possibly go and hold others' debts over them? Especially if doing so leads to my own imprisonment. Harboring unforgiveness harms me and displeases God, so I let it go. And if you want the freedom of forgiveness, you must make this decision, too.

After thinking it through and forgiving, you must intentionally manage this decision. It helps to think of forgiving as a process more than an act. That's because once you decide to forgive, the old feelings don't simply disappear, as wonderful as that would be. The pain, resentment, anger, all of it, eat at you and convince you to detour from your forgiveness decision and reroute yourself to prison. This is why you must devise a strategy to manage this decision.

The one that worked for me is an expanding prayer. My prayers started, *"God, I'm not even willing to be willing, so please make me willing to forgive."* Over time, it moved to *"God, I am willing to forgive, but this is really hard for me; please help."* Eventually, it moved to *"God, I choose to forgive this man, and I release the debt he owed for his sins and my anger with it."*

Though these prayers were sincere, they did not immediately change my feelings. Yet I discovered that if you determine to forgive, your feelings follow, eventually. Within a couple of months, a work of deep healing began that would take much longer to deepen. Eventually, I realized I forgave the man "in my heart" as Jesus desired. Suddenly, I was living lighter.

Imagine carrying 50 pounds of weight wherever you go and setting it down one day. That's how I felt. God wants that same unburdening for you. Talk to Him about the unforgiveness you carry. Talk to a wise friend or trusted counselor. To experience the freedom your soul longs for, you cannot afford to put this off any longer. Freedom grows where forgiveness flows.

Steps to Forgiving:

1. Do the Houses Exercise with someone you trust.

2. Read Matthew 18.

3. Make the decision to forgive -consider the Why.

4. Maintain the decision to forgive—contemplate and practice the How.

5. Choose to forgive fully and let your feelings follow.

Chapter 34—Make Sense of Suffering

His face looked haunted as he stared past us solemnly reflecting on a bitter memory from many decades past. My Pepere's face usually had a smile or a knowing grin and frequently yielded his perfected signature wink. Sure, my grandfather would occasionally get angry and "holla" (in his thick Northeast accent) at the stupid politicians who wound him up and made him yell "for cryin' out loud!" but his default was to be fun and happy. Maybe this is why seeing my typically gregarious grandfather caught in a rare loop of melancholy was so jarring. Yet how would anyone who had experienced what he had react any differently?

He told the story of a beautiful young woman named Rose, to whom he was engaged to be married. One dark, rainy Halloween night (I know it sounds like a ghost story, and it kind of is), she was walking and was struck by a car and killed. As he told the story, you could still see the pain on his face long after the event took place. Does time really heal all wounds?

Suffering is an inevitable part of the human experience from the beginning. I still remember the horrific screams of pain my wife gave as I stood by her side for the birth of our three daughters. I also remember the cries of our little infant daughters, who were suddenly thrust naked from the warm, cozy comforts of the womb into the cold, bright, noisy world. Suffering starts from the beginning of our lives and sucker punches us repeatedly all the way until the day we die. Then, the people who loved us suffer the pain of their loss.

Suffering is inevitable and inconvenient, interrupting the comfortable, ideal lives we planned and hoped for. As a Christian, and especially as a pastor, I also see it as one of the biggest stumbling blocks atheists and agnostics have to the Christian faith.

If God is good, loving, and all-powerful, why does He allow good people to suffer? Have you wrestled with this question? Even if you believe, has this question lodged itself in the back of your mind during difficult times and sowed little seeds of doubt? I have experienced this. And my encouragement to you is not to shove these thoughts from the back of your mind down your throat into some soul black hole, but instead reach for them, pull them to the front of your mind, and work through them.

For years, I medicated the symptoms of my suffering, but eventually, I learned to soberly make sense of my suffering. Each new pain begins a new process that is never easy, but the healing benefits of this are immense. If you have not experienced this yet, I hope you find help in learning what I have learned.

I found that while difficult, it is possible to make sense of suffering when you consider its perpetrator, its path, and its purpose. When bad things happen, we usually blame God for it. On the way to an important pastors' event that I was greatly looking forward to, my tire blew out on the highway. My first reaction was not to thank God for keeping me from crashing due to this sudden danger but instead to angrily demand, *"How could you let this happen when you knew how badly I needed encouragement today?"* Is that fair, though? Do we really think God is sitting on His throne and capriciously blowing out tires or shaking up random things because we failed Him or because He simply wants to mess with us?

Sometimes, bad, unfortunate, and even tragic things happen in an imperfect world. If you study the creation story in Genesis, you see that when sin entered our world, it corrupted nature, human nature, and everything around us, ushering in physical and spiritual death. So sometimes things happen simply due to the current state of our world. Much of your suffering comes through other people who live in this world, be they total strangers or the ones you love the most. And a fair bit of suffering comes from your own hands as the consequences of bad choices, bad habits, and bad company. While it is important to work through this to get your head straight about who caused your suffering, a more helpful and actionable step is to move on to consider what you will do about it.

The path of suffering is the decision you make when suffering stands in front of you like an obstacle in the road of life, blocking the path you hoped to journey upon. Many of us seek to get around suffering and find another route or detour to help us avoid it. These paths have only delayed and even compounded my pain. The detours have always led me back to where I started with the reality that, eventually, I must stop trying to go around suffering and learn to go directly through it.

Our best example of doing this well is Jesus. In the Garden of Gethsemane, His soul was tormented because He knew the suffering of the Cross was right in front of Him. Not only that, the friends he asked to pray for Him fell asleep, so it was just Him and God. Maybe you can relate to how Jesus felt when He said, *"My soul is overwhelmed with sorrow to the point of death."* We need to emulate Jesus' next words: *"My Father, if it is possible, may this cup be taken from me? Yet not as I will, but as you will"* (Matt. 26:39b, NIV).

Did you see that? Even Jesus desired a different path from the terrible suffering in front of Him. God, is there another way? Yet, in the same breath, there was resolved submission and determination to walk through the path of suffering to God's purposes ahead.

You must spend more time on the purpose of suffering than the perpetrator or the path because purpose is essential for us to understand suffering. Rebecca's pain in childbirth was intense, and yet she endured it two more times, naturally with no medication, because to her, the price of the suffering was worth it for the prize of each new baby girl she brought into our family.

It is the same reason Jesus drank the cup of suffering. His death on the Cross secured a remedy for sin and the corruption of our souls, bodies, and world. Grace, forgiveness, redemption, hope, peace, and relational reconnection between lost humanity and the loving Father was restored. In these two examples, choices were made to go forward on the path to suffering to get to greater purpose. In the same way, you have a choice of faith when you are suffering.

Consider this popular verse Paul wrote: *"And we know that God causes everything to work together for the good of those who love God and are called according to his purpose for them"* (Rom. 8:28, NLT).

Jumping back to understanding the perpetrator here, notice that the verse doesn't say "God causes everything" you experience. Stopping the blame game is essential for your well-being, as is understanding what the verse actually says. *"God causes everything to work together for good,"* according to His purposes if you're one of His kids. Bad and hurtful things happen, yet if you trust God, He can bring good of it even if you could never imagine that in the moment.

Many parts of my story were agonizing as I lived them. Yet, in time, God used my experiences when shared with someone who could relate to them, offering them hope. Though we had the joy of having three wonderful daughters, one of our babies didn't make it, as Rebecca suffered a miscarriage. As painful as that was, sharing our experience down that road helped bring other would-be parents who experienced this tragedy a little comfort and empathy in their grief.

Some have said that God never wastes a hurt placed in His hands. God didn't cause the suffering you've walked through, but He can cause good things to come of it if you allow Him. Not only for others but for you, too.

Who is the person you most admire or find interesting? I can almost guarantee that this person endured much suffering in life. In the crucible of pain, your greatest character is forged. "No pain, no gain," declare the muscleheads, and they are correct! Without stressing and tearing your muscles they do not get bigger and more noticeable. In the same way, God uses suffering as a tool to grow you up and develop a depth of character that could not be achieved by any other means. Paul also says this in Romans: *"Not only so, but we also glory in our sufferings, because we know that suffering produces perseverance; perseverance, character; and character, hope"* (Rom. 5:3–4, NIV).

Paul doesn't say you glory in suffering because he's a masochist. He's not after the suffering but what it produces. Want more perseverance in your life? How about greater character? Could anyone use a little more hope? You can pray for these things, but prayer alone does not get you there. These valuable soul assets are only reached by trusting God to walk through the difficult things in life and knowing He will somehow use them for His good purposes for you and the world.

My Pepere married my grandmother and had three beautiful daughters and a bunch of grandchildren, including me.

217

He lived long enough to see me marry Rebecca and to meet our first daughter. He never got to meet the other two. He never got to see the church we planted, to meet the wonderful people who made it such a great church, or to see the many souls there who came to faith in Jesus and will forever be with God in Heaven. While I can't see Pepere ever saying he was glad for what happened to Rose, I can see him smiling in his winsome way at recognizing that God caused it all to work together for good.

Next Steps to Make Sense of Suffering:

1. Consider the perpetrator of suffering -who or what really caused this?

2. Consider the path of suffering -how might suffering be maturing me?

3. Consider the purpose of suffering -what has God done or might do to redeem the suffering I have experienced or observed?

Chapter 35—Remediating Toxic Shame

The pediatric cardiologist told me that because of this disease I was just being told I had, I must be very careful about physical activity. But even so, I was at risk of sudden death at any moment. Lest I had any hopes of beating it, he explained that there was no cure and that I would carry this disease for life. As an adult, I learned about my heart disease, and it is as my doctor assessed, though fortunately, more people die with the disease than from it.

Still, it remains with me, creates limitations, and is something I have to factor into my lifestyle. For the perceptive among you, yes, I have read Act I of this book, and I, too, am shocked I survived after putting my body through all that abuse. This is not the only heart disease I have contended with. There is another that has affected my life greatly at times and restricted me from living to the full. Sadly, you, too, might have this disease. I am speaking of shame, and while not a physical disease, it is a soul disease that, unchecked, can not only limit the growth of wellness in your life, but it can also choke out the vitality you now enjoy.

Perhaps it is important to make a distinction. There is a healthy shame, and the fear of that might prevent you from doing bad things or cause you to feel embarrassed when you do. This shame is usually short-lived and carries a net benefit for you and your community. It also assures you that you are probably not a psychopath, another benefit of shame. The real challenge lies with what Ken Baugh, author of *Unhindered Abundance* (which I highly recommend), describes as toxic shame. He says, *"Toxic shame is an attack on your character, value and worth."* See the difference?

Shame makes you feel bad about something you did, while toxic shame causes you to feel bad about who you are. Whether you put toxic shame on yourself or have let others do that for you, it lodges deep into your heart, distorting your perception of yourself and limiting you and your relationships with those around you. And while it might not destroy your body, and the heart disease of toxic shame won't cause sudden death, it can kill you with a thousand cuts.

On a literal mountaintop in Montana, at a gathering called the Trinity Encounter, I participated in an exercise that awakened me to how deeply and significantly shame operated within me, like undiagnosed high cholesterol. As I shared with the small group of guys in my cabin, we realized this was a common theme among all of us. Each shared the toxic shame that plagued their existence as they described the sources of shame and its deep impact on their souls.

One surprising area to us all was body shame. One guy said, *"I wish guys talked more openly about body shame in the same way that women do."* The vulnerability around the porch was as shocking as it was liberating. There was an odd hope in us that the possibility of living in a newfound freedom was now possible simply by bringing our buried secrets to the surface. I want you to join us in this liberation. It should be noted that some struggle with excessive pride over their physical appearance. If that is you, dear reader, I would encourage you to redirect praise to God rather than yourself and caution you that gravity will catch up with you eventually. Let's return to shame.

Since toxic shame distorts how we view ourselves and others, to experience lasting freedom from it, you need to SEE differently. Yeah, another acronym, but you can laugh now and thank me later when you remember the steps to remediate its toxic effect on your life. Once you detect unhealthy shame in your life, the first thing you need to do is "Stop the production." If you are serious about remediating the destructive forces of toxic shame on your soul, you must also examine your habits, behaviors, and even thought life, to consider if a recurring pattern is providing steady shame production and then mercilessly pursue its elimination.

We deal with thoughts and habits in other chapters, but the key here is you may be constantly feeding the monster within that is killing you. Toxic shame must be starved mercilessly and rendered impotent in you. What I am suggesting will seem very difficult to you, and I'm sure it is. However, living with chronic shame is not easy either, so I'm certain it is worth whatever work you have to put in to do this. Just as you can't outrun a bad diet, you cannot out-heal the steady manufacturing and reinforcement of toxic shame in your life. You must stop the production to give yourself a fighting chance at freedom, but SEEing yourself differently requires even more of you.

To shake its vice grip on your life, you must "Expose the shame." The first couple God created was described as follows: *"Adam and his wife were both naked, and they felt no shame"* (Gen. 2:25, NIV). Beautiful. No fear, no shame, no pretense. Do you remember what Adam and Eve did after they sinned by violating God's one simple instruction to them?

"Then the eyes of both of them were opened, and they realized they were naked; so they sewed fig leaves together and made coverings for themselves. Then the man and his wife heard the sound of the Lord God as he was walking in the garden in the cool of the day, and they hid from the Lord God among the trees of the garden" (Gen. 3:7–8, NIV).

They covered up their naked shame and hid themselves from the God they had enjoyed daily walks with in the garden. Toxic shame distorts you on so many levels. It pushes you to cover up and hide yourself from others with various fig leaf layers and hiding techniques for fear of people seeing what you did and who you really are. Maintaining your cover-up further exhausts an already weary soul. It buries your true self under layers of self-deception and masks. Freedom requires us to push back on old patterns and expose our shame to loosen its death grip.

The last time I relapsed on drugs in early 1996, I felt deeply ashamed that I had done such a stupid thing. My natural reaction was to sweep it under the carpet and not tell anyone.

However, I recognized this was a crossroads moment. I didn't know where the new unknown path would lead me, but I knew full well where the old destructive path was headed, and I wanted no part of that. I told my Christian roommate and my new Christian friends what happened. I laughed when one of my Christian friends passionately rebuked me, *"You can't do that anymore!"* *"I know,"* I said, *"that's why I'm telling on myself."* In an instant, my sin and shame were exposed, and they had no power over me.

I don't know whom you need to expose yourself to, but you need to do it. Start with God. He already knows anyway, and it'll be a good, healing conversation. Then, tell another human. Not everyone, unless you feel comfortable doing so, but expose your deepest shame to someone you trust. Start with a counselor if you aren't ready to talk to a close friend. It is difficult but also so freeing that it will feel like the weight you didn't even realize you carried has been removed from your shoulders. It also sets you up for the final step to SEE past shame.

Once the fig leaves are torn off, and you crawl out from under the rock you've hidden under, it is time to "Embrace the real you." Maybe the toxic shame has something to do with your design or your body. You think of yourself as broken, defective, or a factory mishap. Please read and reread this verse carefully until you can embrace it yourself: *"I praise you because I am fearfully and wonderfully made; your works are wonderful, I know that full well"* (Ps.

139:14, NIV). It might take some time, but learn to accept that God made you intentionally and for His purposes. God makes wonderful things, not garbage, and that includes you!

Maybe your issues are less about your perceived shortcomings and more about sin committed by you or upon you. After Adam and Eve's tough conversation with God that included blame-shifting and excuse-making and consequences for them from God, we see God's grace for His beloved creation: *"The Lord God made garments of skin for Adam and his wife and clothed them"* (Gen. 3:21, NIV).

At first glance, it could seem like God just made a better cover-up for Adam and Eve. That's true, but it also runs deeper. It is believed that to make this clothing, God sacrificed an animal to provide them with proper clothing. This was temporary and foreshadowed an even deeper covering. Isaiah, in the foretelling of Jesus' redemptive work, proclaimed this: *"I delight greatly in the Lord; my soul rejoices in my God. For he has clothed me with garments of salvation and arrayed me in a robe of his righteousness…"* (Isa. 61:10a, NIV).

On the Cross, naked and exposed publicly, Jesus took all of your sin, guilt, and shame on Himself and suffered an excruciating death in your place, and offers an incredible deal. In the greatest exchange possible, you give Jesus all your junk. He gives you grace, forgiveness, salvation, and eternal life and wraps you in His robe of righteousness. So when God looks at the believer in Christ, He doesn't see the wretched sinner you see in the mirror. He looks at you as an upstanding son or daughter, not because of what you have done, but because Jesus removed your shame and covered you in His righteousness.

You must confront the lie that the shameful things you did, or were done to you, are who you are. Instead, embrace that the real you is loved, redeemed, adored, restored, and righteous before God, thanks to Jesus. It takes time to live this out properly, and we will not do that perfectly in this lifetime; fortunately, God has grace for us. The heart disease of toxic shame requires you to live entangled in shame-producing thoughts and actions, to continuously cover up and hide yourself from God, others, and even yourself, and to allow yourself to be defined by your sins and shortcomings. God can help you SEE your way out of this crippling disease when you're ready.

Steps to Deal With Toxic Shame:
1. Stop the production.
2. Expose the shame.
3. Embrace the real you.

Chapter 36—Deal With Your Emotions

In the early days of moving back to Connecticut to start our church, another church-planting friend invited me to a Sunday service to dedicate his baby son. Honored to be asked, I left with plenty of time to make the less than three-hour drive to Long Island. To guide me to my destination, I was sporting the cutting-edge tech of the Garmin PDA/GPS combo with SD cards to power the maps. (Hey, this was 2005. I didn't have a Blackberry, and the iPhone was still a few years away from revolutionizing our lives, so it was pretty incredible then.)

Entrusting my tech to guide me, I went on mental autopilot, listening to worship music, reflecting, rock & roll, an audiobook, etc., as I followed the simple instructions in front of me. As the journey went on, my Spidey sense tingled, and I felt something amiss. A minute later, a sign informed me that I was in New Jersey, which confirmed my fears that I was way off course. My heart rate accelerated as I pulled over, rerouted, and realized I'd now be there just on time rather than very early.

I called my friend, told him, then headed back. Unfortunately, the new route took me dead through the center of New York City, which, even on a Sunday morning, is an insane drive. My new estimated time was 30 minutes late, and the coffee was catching up quickly, but I didn't have time to stop in Manhattan to relieve myself. Soon, my ETA was an hour late, and

I had to tell my friend, who then moved the dedication to the end of the church service. Eventually, I got there, found an outdoor restroom (don't ask), ran in, grabbed the baby, and did the dedication. My problem wasn't a lack of planning; I had trusted the wrong device to navigate me on an important day. Many people do this with their emotions.

A coworker at the first church where I worked used to regularly say, *"Emotions are irrelevant."* I don't agree with that, but there is some truth to what he said. Emotions are a powerful, God-given part of who you are and how you experience life. But they can be a destructive force when used irresponsibly. Like my old GPS, emotions are a terrible navigation system that can take you way off course and put you in places and situations that make life more stressful and chaotic for you and the people around you. I know this from firsthand experience.

When I was younger, my feelings governed my actions with positive and negative emotions. Some of the worst decisions I made in life were deeply visceral and profoundly destructive. As you examine your experience, how true is this of you? Has anger led you to words or actions that embarrassed you, hurt others, and ended relationships? Has shame led you repeatedly back to the thing that caused the shame to begin with? Has fear paralyzed you with worry or caused you to make a foolish decision you later regretted? Is it another emotion? Another unpleasant destination? When emotions steer you, you often find yourself way off course, desperately wishing you weren't lost and hoping to get back on track. Emotions make a terrible guidance system, but they are helpful for something else.

Emotions are best leveraged like the warning signals on your vehicle dashboards that tell you things like your tire pressure is low, fluids need to be refilled, maintenance is required, or even a major malfunction might happen. Emotions might be a terrible tool for direction, but they are an essential part of internal inspection to help you understand what's happening inside. When you drive your car, you ignore the inconvenient warning signals at your peril. You might break down somewhere or permanently damage your car if you push on while the dashboard attempts to tell you something helpful. The same is true if you ignore your emotions, as they are the dashboard in your life that helps you know if something is off, missing, or even if you are about to break down. I've often used my car manual to look up what the dashboard lights mean to understand and address the issue properly. The same is true for you with your emotions. Different emotions signal different things happening deep inside. Sometimes, the emotional catalyst is obvious, but sometimes, it's not as apparent. In such cases, it helps to do a little more digging to get to the root and understand what signals tell you about your current condition.

In his book, *The Voice of the Heart*, Chip Dodd discusses "impairments" or feelings and their corresponding "truths" that reveal the emotion underneath the top layer of emotion or behavior. He also discusses how to receive the "gift" from each as you work through them. For example, underneath any resentment you experience, you feel hurt. Underneath the anxiety you wrestle with is fear. I won't tell you anymore because I don't want to give away too much of his book, nor do I wish for Chip to sue me, but you get it.

Whatever unpleasant emotion you feel has tapped into something deeper going on in your heart, and you'd be wise to investigate what's happening under the hood of your life. The dump truck exercise in chapter 21 might be a helpful investigative tool for you in this process. It might also be wise to enlist a good, experienced counselor to help you not only detect some heart issues that are powerful emotional triggers for you but also help you press into them for deeper healing so the emotions have less power to lead you to destructive reactions of feeling, thought, and action. Until you address root heart issues, trying to deal with the symptoms of lashing out in anger, hiding in shame, wallowing in self-pity, etc., can be a futile and exhausting game of emotional Whack-a-Mole. However, since long-term healing takes time, and some emotions come from sudden, unexpected blows, you'd be wise to work on controlling your emotions in the moment rather than letting them control you.

Proverbs is a book of wise, pithy sayings like this one that is pertinent to our topic: *"Like a city whose walls are broken through is a person who lacks self-control"* (Prov. 25:28, NIV). Not only are you capable of doing incredible damage to others under the influence of unrestrained emotions, but you are exposed and vulnerable when you lack self-control. Since emotions are a key driver for lacking self-control, it is wise to begin developing tactics and a long-term strategy for controlling your emotional impulses and outbursts. Removal and replenishment are your friends here!

I had a friend in the FBI who was a total warrior; his nickname was Chuck Norris. Yet, this battle-tested, intensely trained, and always-armed soldier told me something fascinating about encountering dangerous people. He said your #1 mission is to de-escalate. He was trained to always consider the quickest way to lower temperatures to reduce the chances of a violent interaction. De-escalation is a wise strategy you can use today to help build self-control. The next time you feel that deep emotion burning violently through you, step out of the room and go somewhere where you can cool down and release the pressure. This allows whomever you're interacting with time and opportunity to do the same. This simple step of practicing practical self-control can spare you from lots of pain as you work on developing even deeper self-control in a way that takes more time, but is even more life-changing.

In his letter to the Galatians, Paul tells us: *"But the fruit of the Spirit is love, joy, peace, forbearance, kindness, goodness, faithfulness, gentleness and self-control. Against such things there is no law"* (Gal. 5:22–

23, NIV). Note that fruit isn't manufactured. It is cultivated and grown. Spiritual fruit happens the same way—you can't will it into existence; you simply have to be positioned properly for it to grow in your life. As you read the list, the fruit of the Spirit offers you good qualities for your life, including self-control. So, how do you get positioned for all this great stuff to grow in your life?

Jesus tells us: *"I am the vine; you are the branches. If you remain in me and I in you, you will bear much fruit; apart from me you can do nothing"* (John 15:5, NIV). Simply stay connected to Jesus. You can't produce this fruit alone, but if you actively work on maintaining an intimate relationship with Jesus, one of the many benefits and byproducts will be His producing self-control in your life. When you practice self-control, it is much easier for emotions to be helpful dashboard signals rather than an unreliable navigation system leading you to wild places like New Jersey.

Steps to Deal With Your Emotions:
1. Identify which emotions regularly trip you up the most.
2. Do heart work to explore the root issues under those emotions.
3. Build de-escalation practices into your life for emotionally charged situations.
4. Connect more deeply to Jesus so He can cultivate greater self-control in your life.

Chapter 37—Run With the Right People

The plate of pancakes overflowing with maple syrup awaited on the other side of that goal line, I reminded myself as I dug deep within to find a final burst of energy to push myself over the finish line. Satisfaction and relief overwhelmed me as I ran past the goal line. I hate running, yet I had just completed the New Haven Road Race. Granted, it was only a 5k, and we won't discuss my time, but I finished something I never imagined doing. And I never would have started or completed any of it without the people who ran with me that day.

Whom do you run with? I don't mean physically running, though that's great if you do, but who are the people closest to you? While much of the transformational work in our lives happens between us and God, it also happens in our relationships with the people who have close access to us and vice versa. So, who are those people, and are they the right people? How do you know if they are the right people? The right people will do distinct things to help you become the best version of yourself and prove they're the ones you want to run with.

The people you want to run with will:

Push You Forward

The right people will push you forward in life. Jeff is a lifelong runner who competed in many marathons and road races and is one of my closest friends. He knew I hated running but also knew it would benefit me. While Jeff knew I'd never go for marathon training, he pushed me to enter the road race and begin preparing for it. He steered me to a "From Couch Potato to 5K" app that provided the necessary progressive training. From imagination to preparation, Jeff helped push me to that starting line. Do the people around you push you forward or hold you back? Do they allow you too much complacency, or do they challenge in order to bring out the best in you?

Run Alongside You

Coach Ed was a PE coach committed to training others to maximize physical fitness. When he heard what Jeff had roped me into, he got excited and began showing up at 5:30 a.m. several days a week to run with me and take me through some exercise drills as training for the road race. It wasn't like Rocky, where Coach tied a rope around me, and I had to tow him on a bicycle behind me (though there was an exercise in which I was tied to a car). Instead, Ed did all of the training with me. He ran alongside me.

This is a great way to determine if current friends and prospective ones are the ones you should run with. As you run through life, look over in the lane next to you. Who are the ones who also want to grow? To move forward? Who is running in the same direction or at least a good direction you'd like to run in? It's difficult to be close to someone running in the opposite direction, constantly lagging or running too far ahead of you. So look over in the lanes around you and see who is keeping pace with you.

Slow You Down

I was charged and ready on the day of the race. The sky was sunny and blue, and a refreshing breeze kept things cool. Thousands of people were there to compete in the various races or to cheer on their loved ones. Filled with excitement and energy, I ran hard, and one of my friends remarked, *"Wow, he's running a 6-minute mile."* Coach wasn't very impressed and slowed us all down by saying, *"He won't be able to finish the race if he runs at this pace."* He was right. I had no idea how fast I was running, and I wouldn't have been able to sustain that pace the entire race.

While you want those in your closest circle to push you forward and run alongside you, you also need people to slow you down when necessary. Sometimes, we get ahead of ourselves, keep an unsustainable pace, or move in a direction in which we may not see the pitfalls. It's challenging to confront someone intent on moving a certain way. But the friends we want are the ones who will endure the discomfort for our benefit when necessary.

Spur You On

As the race was nearly finished, my run became a fast walk. Jeff, Coach, and Ismael, who could have easily finished much earlier, slowed their pace to keep in step with me. After allowing some recovery time, they said, *"Bill, look onward. The finish line is just ahead; we're almost there. Let's run and finish strong. You can do it!"* With the goal in sight and the encouragement of my friends, I resumed running and crossed the finish line I thought I'd never reach.

Good friends won't just slow you down when you're off course; they'll also spur you on when you need some encouragement and inspiration to finish what you've set out to do, even when you're exhausted and feel like giving up. Do you have people like that in your life? At least one?

This proverb is an excellent example of how a friend helps us become better: *"As iron sharpens iron, so a friend sharpens a friend"* (Prov. 27:17, NLT).

Notice that a mutual sharpening occurs—a mutual spurring toward greater things in life—not just in what we accomplish but also in who we become. This applies to all the categories of those we want to run with.

Ask yourself, not only are those around you doing these things for you? Are you doing these things for them? To have good friends, we must be good friends in all the areas discussed and one more.

Celebrate Your Wins

The best people around you will not only be there to pick you up when you are down but also to celebrate your wins and successes in life. We've all experienced joy diminished when something good happening to us because someone around us let their envy or jealousy leak out. The friends you want to run with resist those baser temptations and joyfully celebrate with you when good things come your way.

After the race, we went back to Jeff's house with all our families and ate stacked plates of fancy pancakes, endless bacon, sausage, juices, good coffee and more. We feasted like we all ran a marathon, even though it was only a 5k, because my friends believed that my accomplishment, which I never would have attempted or achieved without them, deserved a party. These are the kinds of people you want to run with.

Steps to Running With the Right People:

1. Evaluate your current closest circle by the criteria of good running partners above.

2. Intentionally subtract people taking you in the wrong direction from your closest circle.

3. Carefully add people who will take you in the right direction to your closest circle.

4. Work on becoming the kind of friend to others you would want to have.

Chapter 38—Serve Other People

It was a beautiful Saturday morning, and though it was typically a day off for me, I knew it was important to be out working that day with the guys. Calvary House was in a rundown neighborhood plagued with drugs, prostitution, and various other crimes and shady behavior. This environment provided constant temptation to the residents determined to break away from their past enslavement, constantly flaunting many of their former vices in their faces by proximity. And yet, we marched out into those streets with gloves and garbage bags in teams to clean up all the trash that littered the streets, sidewalks, and lawns as an act of service to our neighbors.

In addition to junk food packages and fast-food bags, we picked up beer bottles, nippers, crack cans, drug baggies, condoms, and other disturbing reminders of the places many of us came from. The appearance of the streets from the beginning and end of the day was a radical contrast, and some neighbors expressed gratitude to us for being out there to beautify their spaces. But why would we take a group of guys trying to get their lives cleaned up to clean up a mess they didn't make in the streets around them?

The obvious answer is to serve the people around us as Jesus instructed and modeled for His followers. Our shadow mission as leaders was to help the guys strike a blow against something inside that must be confronted for true recovery to take root, and to begin to pattern in them something that would serve them and the people in their spheres well throughout their lifetimes. We needed to confront selfishness by focusing them more on serving others than themselves, even while they struggled. We'd all do well to embrace this lesson.

What would you do today if you knew you would die tomorrow? I'd probably have an excellent final meal, surround myself with my closest family and friends, and just try to savor every last moment before I threw off this mortal coil. Jesus, in so many ways, differs greatly from me. The night before He would die, He enjoyed a feast. But it was the Passover meal that symbolized the significance and purpose of His death, which was to sacrifice His life for the salvation of many. As if that wasn't honorable and selfless enough, Jesus did something shocking and very different than most of us would as one of His final lessons to his core followers. He wrapped a towel on His waist, stooped down, and washed His disciples' feet. His followers were shocked as this nasty job (feet got very dirty and rank back then) typically fell to a servant to perform on behalf of their master's guests. In this teachable moment, Jesus said, *"I have set you an example that you should do as I have done for you. Very truly I tell you, no servant is greater than his master, nor is a messenger greater than the one who sent him. Now that you know these things, you will be blessed if you do them"* (John 13:15–17, NIV).

Jesus showed through His humble actions that nobody was above serving others and instructed His true believers to go out and do the same. Jesus knew there was great need in the world. He wanted to make it clear that part of what His followers should be about is blessing others through intentional acts of service. Even the ones that might be considered lowly to others or even themselves. Counterintuitively, Jesus also promised that those who do these things will be blessed. The good feeling you get when you help someone meaningfully is part of that blessing. But the more you serve as a lifestyle, the more it also blesses you by contending with two things that might hold you back: selfishness and insufficiency.

I took a while to realize how selfish my addiction and all the irresponsible behavior that went along with it was. It might shock you to hear that, especially if someone you love is an addict and you've had to endure a lot of unkept promises and obnoxious behavior and even clean up more than a few of their messes. However, when someone is enslaved by addictive behavior, they're desperately trying to drown out their pain at any cost. In so doing they are often blind to the pain they inflict on others, especially those who love them the most.

Selfishness is one of those blind spots for most people, like greed. You rarely encounter someone who says my biggest problem is *"I'm just too greedy"* or *"I'm just too selfish."* However, those things are often obvious to the people around them. Yet once selfishness is recognized within, an inner crisis takes place. You feel guilty and convicted as you recognize how horribly you have behaved and how that affected so many in so many ways.

Serving others doesn't atone for your past sins. But it creates new behavior, which breaks the patterns of selfishness within you as you become a blessing to others. You need not be an addict to be selfish; most of us have abundant selfishness in some form. All you need to do to see it is to get married and watch the sparks fly for the first year as you adjust to living with each other. Your partner will be a great mirror for you as you will be for them.

So, do you wash someone's feet? You can. I once was shocked when a pastor called me in his office and asked me to sit down. He got his shoe polish out, got down, and shined my shoes while I sat in shock. After my shoes glistened and I remained in shock, he smiled and said, *"Don't tell anyone; this is my way of washing feet."* Since I wasn't supposed to say anything, let's keep that story between us. I've never forgotten it because it was an incredible example of someone applying Jesus' lesson. And the reason it was so powerful was because it met a practical need; my shoes looked crappy and then they glistened.

Some churches still hold foot-washing services. I don't mean to knock that because it can provide a valuable lesson in humility. However, people don't need their feet washed the way they did in Jesus' time, yet practical needs abound for the person

241

willing to see them and meet them. Every time you do this you keep your selfishness in check and set the person served and yourself up for a blessing. Some don't hold back from serving because they're selfish; they don't feel like they have much to offer others.

After a year or two of faithfully attending the megachurch I reconnected with Jesus in, my mom asked me, *"When are you going to start serving?"* I was a little astonished because when I saw the size of the church, I assumed that with so many people attending, they had everything covered. My other hesitation was, *What in the world do I have to offer? I'm not that far removed from drugs and debauchery, so how in the world could I really offer anything of value?* On behalf of every pastor or church leader in the world, I want to assure you there's a place for you to serve and make a difference!

Insufficiency also holds many of us back because we erroneously believe we have little to offer someone else. If you are willing, you can always make a difference. My wife is skilled with home improvements and repairs, and I am not. However, I found that I could still be useful. I say, *"I'm not handy, but I do have hands."*

After Hurricane Sandy, a group from our church went on assignment with Samaritan's Purse, serving in an impoverished trailer park ravaged by the storm. Many guys and gals were more skilled than me, but that didn't mean I was useless. I was good at crawling underneath the trailers and ripping out the soaked insulation filled with black mold. I was also good at finding

Jeremy, who was highly skilled when our group leader (who bore more than a passing resemblance to Danny Trejo) needed someone with construction chops. Not only did being there afford me a front-row seat to witness a possum fall onto my friend Chip's face while he worked in a confined, dark space under a trailer, leading him to scream more shrilly than any girl, it also let me serve poor, desperate people in a time of great need despite my lack of skill or experience.

Don't let your inexperience, insecurities, and feelings of inadequacy or insufficiency rob you of the blessing of serving others. There is always a way you can make a difference when you simply make yourself available.

Over the years, the Calvary House developed even deeper connections with our neighbors. We teamed up with the city we were in to build a park where neighboring children could have a nice place to play. We began to hold cookouts, inviting everyone in the neighborhood to come and enjoy a meal with us. We were excited to see some of our guests find hope by connecting or reconnecting with Jesus. The guys in the program learned a valuable lesson in this. Just because they had a past they weren't proud of and were in a situation they would rather not be in, they, too, could feel the joy of making a difference by putting aside selfishness and insufficiency to humbly serve others. Sometimes, it all starts with picking up a piece of trash.

Steps to serve others:

1. Identify any areas of selfishness you see in yourself.

2. Consider the insufficiency and insecurity that holds you back from helping others.

3. Confront your selfishness and insufficiency by performing a small act of service today.

4. Find a place in your community or church where you can regularly serve others.

Chapter 39—Take the Second Chance

Rebecca and I took in the rich, savory scents of the New York City pizza shop we sat in in the mid-2000s while our ears received another interesting capture. Two men, clearly native New Yorkers, sat across from each other catching up on life when one man asked about the other's current dating status. (You absolutely should imagine this dialogue in George and Jerry's voices because it felt like we unknowingly stumbled onto an episode of *Seinfeld*.) *"Are you still dating that girl?"* "Jerry" asked. *"Not a chance,"* "George" casually replied as he explained, *"I found out she's a born-again."* *"A born again?"* his friend asked in surprise. *"Yeah, she's a born-again."* Satisfied with that as a reasonable explanation for the relationship termination, they shook their heads in silence and resumed eating. That moment changed how I, as a pastor in the Northeast, communicated Christianity to people. I often repeated this story as I did so.

When people think of a term like "evangelical," they often immediately associate it with politics. And when people hear the term "born again," they frequently associate it with strangeness. This isn't just their Christian neighbor who is kind of like them; these are the weird ones—the born-agains. While I am fine ceding the term evangelical, I am not comfortable doing so with born-again because it is actually a beautiful picture of life.

The concept and even the term were offered to us by Jesus Himself. A Jewish religious leader named Nicodemus, who had been derided by many of his peers, approached Jesus and shared the positive observations he noticed about Jesus, including that He was sent from God. Jesus, who often seemed to answer questions nobody asked but needed to hear, tells Nicodemus: *"Very truly I tell you, no one can see the kingdom of God unless they are born again"* (John 3:3, NIV). Being born again is a second chance in life, a chance for a do-over, a divine mulligan, if you will. Yet, to be excited about this opportunity that Jesus offers, you must see yourself as in need of being born again and understand what Jesus offers you.

Jesus often taught in the synagogues to the awe of all who listened. On one occasion, someone handed him a scroll of Isaiah, and he read these verses: *"The Spirit of the Lord is on me, because he has anointed me to proclaim good news to the poor. He has sent me to proclaim freedom for the prisoners and recovery of sight for the blind, to set the oppressed free, to proclaim the year of the Lord's favor"* (Luke 4:18–19, NIV).

Jesus ended the reading there rather than continuing to the part about God's judgment. This is telling, as it tips the hand as to why Jesus was there. Jesus left Heaven and came to a bad neighborhood called Earth to save it and rescue its inhabitants. Jesus taught not only in the synagogues but also in the mountaintops, the cities, the villages, and wherever listening ears needed hope. Jesus had harsh words reserved for the religious leaders who followed the law but were corrupt and oppressive in their hardened hearts.

Jesus risked his reputation by going places and hanging out with people that decent people would be offended by. Jesus did not judge the beggars, the lepers, the prostitutes, the tax collectors, or all the despised and marginalized. Instead, He was a hope-dealer to everyone who needed it.

When Jesus closed that Isaiah scroll, he said, *"Today this scripture is fulfilled in your hearing."* In this shocking declaration, Jesus made it clear that He was the Savior, sent by God, who had long been promised in Old Testament scriptures to come and save Israel and the world.

Many didn't believe Jesus because they misunderstood his mission, were too proud to recognize their need for saving, or couldn't believe that the Rescuer from God stood before them as a humble man. Some were cool with Jesus but settled for far less than He offered them. To be ready for all Jesus offers, we need to see ourselves as He does, spiritually destitute ("poor"), captive and broken ("oppressed"), and wounded with limited vision ("blind"). To such a person, Jesus offers revelation ("good news"), redemption ("freedom"), and restoration ("recovery"). You must understand you need rescue before you are willing and ready to be rescued.

Jesus isn't an addition to your portfolio to offer afterlife insurance as a hedge. He is the one you've been waiting for, even as you sought what He offers in various dead-end routes, destinations, and fellow travelers, to make sense of life, death, and suffering and offer you hope, salvation, and a bright future.

So how does it work? How does one become rescued or saved? Paul sums it up this way: *"If you declare with your mouth, 'Jesus is Lord,' and believe in your heart that God raised him from the dead, you will be saved"* (Rom. 10:9, NIV).

As a second chance in life, salvation is as simple as faith in who Jesus is, what He has done for you, and choosing to trust your entire life, to bet the farm, if you will, on Him. After all, what else is an appropriate response to one who died naked and violently on the Cross to take your place, atone for all you've ever done wrong, and offer you forgiveness, a restored relationship with God the Father, a place in Heaven, and His presence and redemptive help here and now? To one who took His life back three days later on the glorious day of His resurrection, showing us that new life, even when things looked hopeless, is available to all who trust and follow Him? If you believe in your heart and make a profession of faith with your mouth, you can be rescued right now and get a second chance at life with Jesus.

Is it really that easy? I love how the Message paraphrase of the Bible puts the verse just a few away from the prior one: *"Everyone who calls, 'Help, God!' gets help"* (Rom.10:13, MSG).

You want help? Call out to God, and it's yours for the taking.

If you are ready to call out to God for help now, and I hope you are if you have never done this, then I'd like to offer a prayer to give you some guidance. Feel free to add to it and talk to God in your own words, but here it is:

Dear God,

I come before you spiritually destitute, a prisoner of many bad habits, broken and busted up, wounded and badly in need of vision for life, and just an all-around sinful person. I'm thankful that even though you knew the worst in me, you wanted to bring out the best in me, save, forgive, redeem, and restore me, and so you sent Jesus to die in my place. Thank you, Jesus, for dying so that I might live, raising yourself from the dead to offer me a new resurrection life, and promising to return for me someday. God, I believe in all this and put my faith and trust in you today. Help me understand and live afresh in the salvation you are granting me right now. Thank you for loving me so much, and I love you back.

In Jesus' name,

_____ (Your name, he knows, but let's keep it personal!)

If you said that prayer, congratulations on the best decision you ever made, and welcome to the family of God. The rest of your show/story has now changed forever for the better.

Epilogue: Closing Curtain

Close calls are often wake-up calls. After I left the church we had ministered to for more than 18 years, I felt lost, displaced, confused, and terrified about what could be next. After several months, I became weary of navel-gazing and, truthfully, quite bored, as I love to be busy and productive. Without a clear direction, my default was to return to sales for a company where I used to work. Within the first week, I began to sense that this might not be the right step, but I had just started so I refused to quit so soon.

Six weeks later, on the way to a sales appointment, a driver turned in front of me as I traveled at 50 mph (the speed limit). It happened so quickly that I had no time to brake or react. The only thing I managed to do was scream as the cars made impact, and I saw a flash of pink haze as the airbags deployed and my car spun around. It was a moment of terror as I was certain I would die. But to my amazement, the car stopped, and I exited my vehicle with minor injuries. The other driver and I were both in shock and both fortunate to be alive.

In an instant, I knew I would never return to that job I was hiding out in, because I knew that for God to have spared me, it meant He wasn't done with me on Earth yet. He still had a purpose and a plan for my life, even if that was unclear. I now know that part of that purpose is sharing my story with others.

Recently, at a friend's church, I gave a message publicly expressing some ideas about this book for the first time. I titled the message "The Rest of Your Story" because my book title hadn't been released, and the title sounded weird with no context or explanation. To be honest, I was a little nervous to share that message. I've preached probably close to 1,000 times in my life, so I wasn't nervous about teaching or even public speaking. Still, I felt the weight of this because though I'm often vulnerable when delivering messages, I rarely put myself out there this much. And though I believe God called me to write this book, I wondered how some of what I had to say and share would be received by other people. I could tell by the audience's laughter, tears, and "amens" as I spoke that I struck a chord and connected with many people.

However, what surprised me was the conversations I had with people after the service. People were kind and told me how moved and encouraged they were by hearing about Jesus' power to change us and by my story as an example. But they also did something else that I didn't expect. They began to share their stories with me. They told of very dark places they'd been in and excruciating experiences they endured. They also told me how God guided, or in some cases is guiding them, through chapters of pain and heartbreak. I came to encourage and give hope, yet many people I spoke with offered that to me.

That is the power of sharing your story. By sharing your brokenness and wounds, along with the breakthroughs and triumphs and what led you there, your story can inspire hope and transformative change in someone else's story. So please don't bottle it up and keep it to yourself.

Maybe you don't have a crazy story like mine, or maybe my story looks tame compared to the wild ride you've been on. That doesn't matter. The world is a rough place, and none of us get out unscathed, so you have something to contribute to the conversation. I hope that something in this book inspired or equipped or encouraged you. If so, maybe send me a message to let me know or write a review. And I encourage you to share your story with someone who may benefit from seeing your scars while their wounds are fresh.

And please don't forget that whether you are in the early spring phase of your life journey or even deep into late winter, the fact that you're breathing today means God still wants to tell some of His story through your life. If I could put my hands on your shoulders and look you in the eyes right now, I'd shake you just a little and smile as I told you with a sense of great urgency that needn't involve a car crash, "Wake up! Your story isn't over!"

May God give you grace as you press into Him for all He has for you and may the redemptive arc of your life be ever stronger and more vibrant for the rest of your show!

References

American History X. Directed by Tony Kaye. Written by David McKenna. Produced by John Morrissey. New Line Cinema, 1998.

Anonymous. *Go Ask Alice.* Edited by Beatrice Sparks. Prentice Hall, 1971.

Beavis and Butt-Head. Created by Mike Judge. MTV, 1993–1997; 2011; 2022–present.

Blizzard Entertainment. *Diablo IV.* Blizzard Entertainment, 2023.

Bradbury, Ray. *The Martian Chronicles.* Doubleday, 1950.

Calhoun, Adele Ahlberg. *Spiritual Disciplines Handbook: Practices That Transform Us.* InterVarsity Press, 2005.

Cops. Created by John Langley and Malcolm Barbour. Premiered on Fox, 1989. Currently produced by Langley Productions.

Cracked. Published by Major Magazines (1958–1985), Globe Communications (1985–2000), and Modern Humor Media (2006–present).

Crazy. Published by Marvel Comics. 1973–1983.

Dodd, Chip. *The Voice of the Heart: A Call to Full Living.* Sage Hill Resources, 2001.

Drugstore Cowboy. Directed by Gus Van Sant. Screenplay by Gus Van Sant and Daniel Yost. Produced by Karen Murphy. Distributed by Avenue Pictures, 1989.

Friday the 13th. Created by Victor Miller and Sean S. Cunningham. Paramount Pictures, 1980–present.

Friends. Created by David Crane and Marta Kauffman. Warner Bros. Television, 1994–2004.

Goodfellas. Directed by Martin Scorsese. Produced by Irwin Winkler. Screenplay by Nicholas Pileggi and Martin Scorsese. Warner Bros., 1990.

Hollywood Sun-Tattler. Published by E.W. Scripps Company. 1942–1991.

Iron Maiden. *Flight of Icarus.* Directed by David Mallet. Music video. Released by EMI Records, 1983.

Iron Maiden. *Run to the Hills.* Directed by David Mallet. Music video. Released by EMI Records, 1982.

Lewis, C.S. *Mere Christianity.* HarperOne, 1952.

MAD Magazine. Published by EC Comics. 1952–present.

Marilyn Manson & The Spooky Kids. *Grist-o-Line.* Self-released, 1990.

Marilyn Manson. *Portrait of an American Family.* Produced by Trent Reznor, Marilyn Manson, and Roli Mosimann. Nothing Records/Interscope Records, 1994.

Marvel Comics. *What If...?* First published February 1977. Various writers and artists.

McDowell, Josh, and Sean McDowell. *Evidence That Demands a Verdict: Life-Changing Truth for a Skeptical World.* Thomas Nelson, 1972.

McDowell, Josh, and Sean McDowell. *More Than a Carpenter.* Tyndale House Publishers, 1977.

Metallica. *Master of Puppets.* Produced by Flemming Rasmussen and Metallica. Elektra Records, 1986.

Office, The. Developed by Greg Daniels. NBC, 2005–2013.

Osbourne, Ozzy. *"Crazy Train."* Track 2 on *Blizzard of Ozz.* Jet Records, 1980.

Over the Edge. Directed by Jonathan Kaplan. Produced by George Litto and Harold Schneider. Orion Pictures, 1979.

Peterson, Eugene H. *The Message: The Bible in Contemporary Language.* Colorado Springs: NavPress, 2002.

Pink Floyd. *The Wall.* Produced by Bob Ezrin, Roger Waters, and David Gilmour. Harvest Records, 1979.

Return of the Jedi. Directed by Richard Marquand. Produced by Howard G. Kazanjian, George Lucas, and Rick McCallum. Lucasfilm Ltd., 1983.

Scazzero, Peter. *Emotionally Healthy Spirituality: It's Impossible to Be Spiritually Mature, While Remaining Emotionally Immature.* Zondervan, 2014.

Seinfeld. Created by Larry David and Jerry Seinfeld. NBC, 1989–1998.

Silence of the Lambs, The. Directed by Jonathan Demme. Screenplay by Ted Tally. Produced by Kenneth Utt, Edward Saxon, and Ron Bozman. Orion Pictures, 1991.

Star Wars. Created by George Lucas. Lucasfilm Ltd., 1977–
   present.

Sun-Sentinel. Published by Tribune Publishing. 1910–present.

Thief in the Night, A. Directed by Donald W. Thompson. Written
   by Russell S. Doughten Jr. and Jim Grant. Produced by
   Donald W. Thompson. Mark IV Pictures, 1972–1983.

Tyndale House Publishers, ed. *Holy Bible, New Living Translation.*
   Carol Stream, IL: Tyndale House Publishers, 2015.

Young and the Restless, The. Created by William J. Bell and Lee
   Phillip Bell. CBS, 1973–present.

Zondervan, ed. *Holy Bible, New International Version.* Grand Rapids,
   MI: Zondervan, 2011.

Reading Plan for Small Groups and Book Discussions

The Rest of the Man's Show works great for small group discussion, but for maximum effectiveness we recommend this alternative reading and study schedule which preserves the narrative sequentially while grouping the topics thematically:

Week 1 -Chapters: Introduction, Preface, 1, 2, 33 & 34

Week 2 -Chapters: 3, 4, 21 & 36

Week 3 -Chapters 5, 28 & 35

Week 4 -Chapters: 6 & 39

Week 5 -Chapters 7, 24 & 29

Week 6 -Chapters 8, 9, 23 & 32

Week 7 -Chapters 10, 11, Interlude #1 & 31

Week 8 -Chapters 12 & 27

Week 9 -Chapters 13, 14 & 38

Week 10 -Chapters 15, 17 & 22

Week 11 -Chapters 16, 18 & 37

Week 12 -Chapters 19, 20, Interlude #2, 25, 30 & Epilogue

Visit Http://Restofthemansshow.com for a FREE group discussion guide and other resources.

Contacting and Connecting

If this book encouraged or helped you in some way, Bill would love to hear about it. Email him at bill@restofthemansshow.com.

To inquire about Bill speaking at your church or organization's event, or for personal or organizational coaching, email bill@restofthemansshow.com

An online review from wherever you purchased this book and a recommendation to a friend go a long way and are greatly appreciated!

Join Bill's newsletter to stay up to date on upcoming projects at Http://Restofthemansshow.com.